THE

THE RAPTURE

by

Phil Layton

Salvation Books
The Salvation Army International Headquarters
London, United Kingdom

First published 2009
© 2009
The General of The Salvation Army

ISBN 978-0-85412-796-2

Cover design by Nathan Sigauke

Published by Salvation Books
The Salvation Army International Headquarters
101 Queen Victoria Street, London EC4V 4EH, United Kingdom

Printed by UK Territory Print & Design Unit

'We believe that it is the privilege of all believers to be wholly sanctified, and that their whole spirit, and soul, and body may be preserved blameless until the coming of our Lord Jesus Christ.'

The Salvation Army, Doctrine 10

'May God himself, the God of peace, sanctify you through and through. May your whole spirit, soul and body be kept blameless at the coming of our Lord Jesus Christ.
The one who calls you is faithful and he will do it.'

1 Thessalonians 5:23-24

With immense gratitude and eternal love to
Karen, Anastasia and Joshua

About the author

Captain Phil Layton has been studying biblical eschatology since 1988, when he was introduced to the subject by his parents, Majors Kingsley and Margarita Layton. At the time, Phil was unaware of when God's calling would come, and where it would take him, but throughout the years his eschatological studies have increased his love of God, the Bible and The Salvation Army. Since becoming a Salvation Army officer he has written two books which rely on the authority of Scripture texts alone, and which both highlight the importance of having a personal relationship with Jesus Christ. The first of these was *The Sacraments and the Bible*, published in 2007 by The Salvation Army in the United Kingdom, the second is this publication. Phil has a dual appointment within The Salvation Army; serving with his wife, Karen, as corps officer (church pastor) in Hythe, UK, as well as being a Tutor in New Testament Studies at William Booth College, London. In addition, Phil is a corresponding member of The Salvation Army's International Doctrine Council, and a member of its Moral and Social Issues Council in the United Kingdom. He enjoys taking a prominent role in the local Churches Together District Council, and finds greatest fulfilment proclaiming the gospel of Christ. Prior to become an officer, Phil was a computer presentations designer. He has vocational qualifications in management and information technology, a BA degree (Religious Studies) from the University of Kent, and a Master of Theology degree from Heythrop College, University of London, in which he focused on uses and abuses of the Bible, ethics and the Gospels.

Contents

A *Concise Oxford Dictionary Definition*:
Rapture: noun (esp. theol.) act of transporting a person from one place to another (esp. heaven).

Foreword

Jesus is coming again! The event is known as *The Rapture*, taken from the Latin word *raptus* in the Vulgate translation of 1 Thessalonians 4:17. In Greek, the word is *harpazo*, which means 'caught up'or 'taken away'.

Throughout the history of the Church, Christians have affirmed their belief in the return of Jesus – often referred to as The Second Coming. The Rapture – the initial episode of Jesus' return – is a prophesied event in which Christians are instantly taken from earth to be with Jesus. Christians who have died are to be united with their resurrected bodies to participate in this event. The basis for this belief is found in Paul's first recorded epistle, 1 Thessalonians 4:15-17, in which the apostle cites 'the word of the Lord' concerning the return of Jesus to gather his saints:

> 'According to the Lord's own word, we tell you that we who are still alive, who are left till the coming of the Lord, will certainly not precede those who have fallen asleep. For the Lord himself will come down from Heaven, with a loud command, with the voice of the archangel and with the trumpet call of God, and the dead in Christ will rise first. After that, we who are still alive and are left will be caught up together with them in the clouds to meet the Lord in the air. And so we will be with the Lord forever.'

Although all Christian denominations believe in Christ's return to earth, there are three primary views regarding the timing and nature of his return in relationship to the thousand-year (millennial) reign of Christ: Amillennialists (such as Roman Catholics, and others), Postmillennialists (such as Presbyterians, and others), and Premillennialists (such as Baptists, and others). Premillennialists are further divided concerning the the timing of the event. By definition, they believe that the Rapture will take place *before* Christ's Millennial Reign. They are, however, divided on whether the event comes before, midway through, or after the Great Tribulation.

All passages regarding the return of Christ, such as Matthew 24:29-31; 1 Thessalonians 4:15-17 and Revelation 1:7, describe the return of Jesus in the clouds amid trumpets, angelic activity, heavenly signs, a resurrection, and a gathering of saints. Although some take this event to be figurative, rather than literal, the three groups listed above maintain that passages regarding the return of Christ describe a single event, and that the 'word of the Lord' cited by Paul in 1 Thessalonians 4:15-17 is the Olivet Discourse which Matthew separately describes in Matthew 24:29-31.

The Salvation Army has intentionally not taken an official position on the timing of Christ's return in relationship to both the Great Tribulation and Christ's Millennial Reign. The Salvation Army's handbook of doctrine, presently titled *Salvation Story*, affirms in Appendix 10, under *Interpretations of the Return of Christ*: 'The Salvation Army has avoided speculation about details of the return of Christ. Salvationists prefer to emphasise the Christian responsibility to live in a state of expectation and hope. We should be constantly open to the presence and judgment of God in Christ, and fully involved in the mission of God for the salvation of the world.'

After detailing a number of differing views, the appendix concludes: 'So many differing interpretations suggest that the Bible leaves us with the mystery of God and his purposes for us, which are finally beyond speculation. Our best response is to be silent before the mystery, confident before the promise and trusting before a loving God revealed to us in Jesus Christ.'

My esteemed colleague and friend, Captain Phil Layton, has grappled with the differing views concerning the events surrounding the long anticipated return of Jesus to rapture his people. A valued corresponding member of the International Doctrine Council, Phil Layton has presented a clear and compelling study, approaching the topic with understanding and respectful consideration for all points of view.

May the readers of this commendable book rejoice in the central fact of the Lord's imminent return. As the apostle Paul reminds us in 1 Corinthians 15:51-53 (*NIV*):

> 'Listen, I tell you a mystery: We will not all sleep, but we will all be changed - in a flash, in the twinkling of an eye, at the last trumpet. For the trumpet will sound, the dead will be raised imperishable, and we will be changed. For the perishable must clothe itself with the imperishable, and the mortal with immortality. When the perishable has been clothed with the imperishable, and the mortal with immortality, then the saying that is written will come true: "Death has been swallowed up in victory. Where, O death, is your victory? Where, O death, is your sting?" The sting of death is sin, and the power of sin is the law. But thanks be to God! He gives us the victory through our Lord Jesus Christ.'

This is the Word of the Lord!

**William W. Francis, Commissioner,
Chairman, International Doctrine Council**

The crucial question

The Rapture is a highly debated doctrine. It is demanding an increasingly significant and defined response as greater numbers of people, both within the Church and without, become aware of it. Much has been said about the Rapture, in books, on the internet, in 'end-time' magazines and even in films and documentaries. A variety of opinions can be heard. Together with influences from best-selling fictional stories to media reports, these can sway the emphasis of Church teaching on the subject. Therefore the question addressed in this book is: 'What does the Bible say about the Rapture?' If we try to ignore all the non-biblical material, is there any evidence for a Rapture?

This book offers only a basic introduction to eschatology. It sets the end-time context by briefly interpreting its key themes, but the focus is on the scriptural validity of the Rapture. Specifically the question asked is whether there is any such thing, biblically speaking, or has the Bible merely been used, (or abused), to present an argument for a future event that does not actually exist within God's prophetic plan?

If the evidence of the Bible leads us to conclude that there is such a thing as a Rapture, is there enough biblical information to develop a sustainable view as to its timing, nature and relevance to us today?

Some say the Rapture belongs within a category of teaching too obscure to be taught or preached, due to its diverse interpretations and opinions. Others are content to declare that it belongs to prophetic teaching in general, alongside that of the second coming of Jesus Christ. Some believe it to be so intertwined with the Book of Revelation that any attempt to expound the topic to a congregation is almost bound to be too complex to attempt. Others believe an explanation of 'last things', including the Rapture, should at least be attempted, otherwise a small but significant portion of God's Word is being ignored.

Such attempts, however, are relatively rare. Perhaps this is because some Christian leaders are worried that by introducing the subject they might introduce confusion and misunderstanding. Others may doubt whether eschatology is a relevant part of the gospel to preach today. As a result, many Christians feel either that everything will always continue as it currently is, or that Christ's second advent will be clearly heralded by dramatic signs. They believe that these will enable Christians to turn their attention to it at the appropriate time. Such signs might include the battle of Armageddon, the gospel being spread through every nation, the abomination of desolation and the mark of the beast.

However, if Christ's return is not to be heralded by such events, then it is vital that the world's people be awakened to this fact. If there is a possibility that the next major event in God's eternal plan is imminent, with no reason for delay and no further criteria to be met, then it is essential that Christians should be prepared for it. We should be alerting the rest of the Church and the rest of the world. If there is solid biblical evidence for the Rapture, there should be a heightened zeal and urgency both for living a sanctified life and for evangelisation. Belief in an imminent Rapture simultaneously creates a passion for holiness and salvation.

Therefore, bearing all these factors in mind, this book will attempt to answer the crucial question: does the Rapture concept have a solid Bible-based premise, and, if so, what is its relevance to us today?

Throughout the book the *New International Version* (*NIV*) has been used for all biblical quotations. It is always helpful to read additionally the full context.

'The grass withers and the flowers fall, but the word of our God stands forever'

Isaiah 40:8

Setting the eschatological scene

This first of three larger sections helps set the eschatological scene. It is also divided into three, starting with a chapter containing the key themes and definitions of terms found within this branch of eschatology. It includes an outline of the method of interpretation adopted. The second chapter within this section considers how the Rapture would fit within God's story as found in the Bible. It asks whether such an event would be in keeping with his authorship. The third chapter provides a precise definition of the Rapture, along with its key Scripture texts. It challenges us to assess its plausibility by comparing it to similar past events. The chapter concludes with a brief outline of the differences between those who believe in it.

Definitions, interpretations, and considerations

If studying eschatology, or more specifically the Rapture, is a new concept to the reader, it is vital to understand that this is a difficult topic to teach. This is because it is referring to God's intervention in a dramatic, miraculous way. This kind of intervention has not been recorded since the Holy Spirit came on the day of Pentecost back in the first century (Acts 2).

In addition, it is not easy to delve into one aspect of eschatology, such as the Rapture, without referring to other eschatological terms and themes.These may be equally new in concept and at times intimidating because of their apocalyptic nature.

Readers should therefore remember that the Rapture is not something of which Christians should be afraid. When we consider what the future may hold we know that it is our Heavenly Father who holds the future. Nothing is beyond his control. He is to be trusted, and he will do only what is best for us. When Christians begin the journey of discovery into what Scriptures teach regarding the end-times they can do so with the full assurance of being blessed and encouraged.

Even the somewhat alarming Book of Revelation begins:

'Blessed is the one who reads the words of this prophecy, and blessed are those who hear it and take to heart what is written in it, because the time is near.'

Revelation 1:3

If you have placed your trust in Jesus Christ's death and resurrection to reconcile you to God then biblical eschatology is a subject full of blessing, encouragement and assurance. We need have no fear of what is to come. Proponents of the Rapture assert that it provides the Christian with an even greater reason to face the future with joyful expectation, rather than fear.

A simple rule for interpreting prophecy

When we interpret biblical prophecy we are attempting to find out what the Author of that prophecy was trying to say. Unless the text specifically claims to be a mystery, deliberately unfathomable, we can assume it was written in order to be understood at some point. So it is right to begin our approach to such Scripture texts by assuming they may be interpreted within their literal meaning, unless the context, and the study of related Scripture, suggests otherwise. This means that any text which makes sense as it stands should not automatically be re-interpreted or given a higher meaning. Only if its meaning is ambiguous should it be interpreted in the light of other Scripture.

6

Eschatology

One definition of eschatology is 'the study of things pertaining to Heaven and Hell, death and judgment'. This book defines it more prophetically as the study of the end-times, the last days, when matters of Heaven, Hell, judgment and death may be ultimately determined. It includes a study of the prophecies regarding the details of these events, including the characters, society and even the politics and religion of the era leading up to the final judgment.

'Son of man,' he said to me, 'understand that the vision concerns the time of the end.'

Daniel 8:17

This book understands eschatology as the study of 'the time of the end'. In this study it is just as important to acknowledge what we *cannot* know, as it is to reveal what we *may* now comprehend.

The revelation of Jesus Christ

The last book of the Bible gets its name from the Greek *apocalypsis*, meaning 'unveiling'. This wonderful part of the biblical library is indeed 'the unveiling of Jesus Christ', revealing his present and future glory. It is important to acknowledge that there are various scholarly ways of interpreting its content, as well as countless ways in which the book has been abused.

There are four standard methods of interpreting Revelation.

The **preterist** view maintains that the work belongs solely to the very early Church, with its descriptions relating to events that occurred at that time. The book therefore has no future or predictive quality, and the events described in it do not relate to the 'times of the end'.

The **historicist** view interprets the Book of Revelation as relating to events throughout history from the time it was written until the time of the interpreter. Throughout the intervening 2,000 years the meaning of events may therefore change as new things happen.

The **idealist** method does not regard the events in the Book of Revelation as describing or predicting any historical or future events at all, but as symbolising the spiritual warfare on earth and in Heaven between good and evil, which will ultimately come to a climax on Christ's return.

The **futurist** view takes the Book of Revelation at face-value unless the text plainly indicates otherwise. By doing so it becomes evident that the events described in it are prophetic and relating to the future. While taking into account the historical setting in which it was written, the futurist interpretation considers chapter four onwards, in particular, to be dealing with matters of the future. This book takes the futurist view.

After this I looked, and there before me was a door standing open in Heaven. And the voice I had first heard speaking to me like a trumpet said, 'Come up here, and I will show you what must take place after this.'

Revelation 4:1

The Rapture

The Rapture is the topic of this whole book and will be defined in detail in a later chapter. For now it may simply be described as the belief that there will be a future event, biblically prophesied, when God will take Christians to be with him in Heaven. Believers who have already died will be taken first, immediately followed by those still alive. This event is separate from the Second Coming of Jesus Christ. The former involves Christians being taken from earth to be with Christ, the latter involves Christ coming back to rule on earth. The timing of the Rapture will be detailed in a later chapter.

Antichrist

An antichrist is anyone who opposes Jesus Christ. The actual word 'antichrist' appears only in the letters of John *(1 John 2:18; 2:22, 4:3; 2 John 1:7)*. However, in eschatological terms this word is often used to describe a real person. He is an individual who is predicted to become very persuasive and powerful, both politically and religiously. He will ultimately be so possessed by Satan himself as to present to the world a counterfeit Christ. He will even have a 'helper' known as the wonder-working 'false prophet' *(Revelation 16:13)*. Between them will exist an evil trinity of Satan, the antichrist and the false prophet *(Revelation 20:10)*. Other titles given to this character include 'the beast' *(Revelation 13:1)*, 'the ruler who will come' *(Daniel 9:26)*, and 'the lawless one' *(2 Thessalonians 2:8)*, among many other names which help describe his attributes. Given his relationship with the devil and his contrast to everything Christlike it will be no surprise that he comes to power through deceit.

The coming of the lawless one will be in accordance with the work of Satan displayed in all kinds of counterfeit miracles, signs and wonders, and in every sort of evil that deceives those who are perishing.

2 Thessalonians 2:9, 10

The Bible tells us that halfway through a seven-year covenant he will break his promises, blaspheme God, and exalt himself, causing an abomination at the Jewish Temple in the process *(Daniel 9:27)*. All of this will help the Jews to recognise him as the deceiver, and simultaneously recognise Jesus Christ as the one and only Saviour.

From this and other Scripture we can know that the antichrist will not be identified until the seven-year Tribulation is to begin. Even then only those with knowledge of biblical prophecy will identify him, while the rest of the nations may well be impressed by his covenant-making abilities.

Israel

In this book references to Israel literally mean Israel and the Jewish people. Some scholars have taken eschatological references to Israel as symbolising the Church. References to the Church and to Israel should be distinguished and are not interchangeable.

Gentiles

Throughout this book the word Gentile simply refers to anyone who is not a Jew. In addition the term non-Jew is sometimes used.

The Tribulation

This term refers to a future seven-year period.

'Seventy "sevens" are decreed for your people and your holy city to finish transgression, to put an end to sin, to atone for wickedness, to bring in everlasting righteousness, to seal up vision and prophecy and to anoint the most holy. Know and understand this: From the issuing of the decree to restore and rebuild Jerusalem until the Anointed One, the ruler, comes, there will be seven "sevens", and sixty-two "sevens". It will be rebuilt with streets and a trench, but in times of trouble. After the sixty-two "sevens", the Anointed One will be cut off and will have nothing. The people of

the ruler who will come will destroy the city and the sanctuary. The end will come like a flood: War will continue until the end, and desolations have been decreed. He will confirm a covenant with many for one "seven". In the middle of the "seven" he will put an end to sacrifice and offering. And on a wing [of the temple] he will set up an abomination that causes desolation, until the end that is decreed is poured out on him.'

Daniel 9:24-27

The Book of Daniel is often considered to be the Old Testament counterpart to Revelation. In it the angel Gabriel specified that God had set a time for his plans to be fulfilled. He had set a time-frame for his people, the Jews, to accept his salvation, and that there was a period of 490 years (70 times seven) in which his dealings with Israel would be fully accomplished, prior to the Second Coming of Jesus Christ.

This 490 years is often described as Daniel's 70 'weeks' of years. The word 'week' is simply used to convey a group of seven in the same way that a 'pair' denotes a group of two, and a 'dozen' denotes a group of 12. That one 'week' of years is equivalent to seven years is evidenced by the fact that the one who will come and 'set up an abomination' on a wing of the Jewish Temple does so in the middle of one of these weeks *(Daniel 9:27).* This character is the one who opposes Christ, and is the antichrist, or the beast. Half-way through the Tribulation period (which is described through Revelation 6:1-19:21) he throws off his peaceful mannerisms and exerts his authority along with his blasphemies for 42 months, which is half of seven years.

'The beast was given a mouth to utter proud words and blasphemies and to exercise his authority for forty-two months. He opened his mouth to blaspheme God, and to slander his name and his dwelling place and those who live in heaven. He was given power to make war against the saints and to conquer them. And

11

*he was given authority over every tribe, people, language and
nation'*

Revelation 13:5-7

As Gabriel divided that time period into two main parts, so shall
we: 483 years equals seven sevens and 62 sevens *(Daniel 9:25).*

This time-frame accurately predicts the gap between the issuing of
King Artaxerxes' edict, in his 20th year, allowing the rebuilding of
Jerusalem *(Nehemiah 2:1-8),* and the crucifixion of Christ, which
is when the Anointed One was 'cut off' *(Daniel 9:26).*

The remaining seven years starts with the confirming of a
covenant *(Daniel 9:27),* and in God's timescale marks a future
period of Tribulation. This is predicted in detail through
Revelation 6:1 – 19:21 as being God's time of wrath upon the
earth. However, it is a wrath which is designed to shake the
securities of humankind. It will allow the gift of freewill once
more to be exercised in the hope that the nations will humble
themselves, acknowledge God and come to him through faith in
Jesus Christ.

This extreme plan of action will be seen to work as many Christians
will be brought to faith during this time. Many Jews in particular
will finally recognise Jesus to be their Lord and Saviour. These
seven years are defined as the years of 'Tribulation' (a word the *NIV*
mentions only in Revelation 7:14), which were previously foretold
by the angel Gabriel in Daniel 9:27. The first group of 483 years has
been accurately fulfilled, so there is no reason to doubt that the
remaining seven years will likewise be literally fulfilled too.

It is as though God has a stop-watch which has been ticking while
he attends to his chosen race, the Israelites, but which was
stopped at the Crucifixion, after which the gospel became
accessible to the Gentiles too. Since the Holy Spirit's dramatic

entry at Pentecost another stopwatch was started, this time for the Gentiles, and God is choosing his perfect timing to bring this Church-age to a close. It is a matter of speculation when the stopwatch for the Jews will recommence and the final seven years be fulfilled.

Of course, anyone can come to God at any time, whether Jew or Gentile, but it is evident that there have been eras when he has focused his purposes on one group with more emphasis than another.

Romans 11 is an important chapter in this respect, and valuable to anyone who needs convincing that God has not finished with the Jews. Particularly noteworthy is verse 25: *'I do not want you to be ignorant of this mystery, brothers, so that you may not be conceited: Israel has experienced a hardening in part until the full number of the Gentiles has come in.'*

Once this number, and its timing, known only to God, comes to pass, then the remaining seven years of Israel's 490 will begin.

For now it is enough to say that the time of the Tribulation's beginning is not knowable, except to say that it begins with the antichrist confirming a covenant. However, the timing of the Rapture in relation to the Tribulation period is extremely pertinent to this study. This subject will be picked up again after analysing whether the Rapture is biblically plausible.

The Second Coming of Jesus Christ

Just as man is destined to die once, and after that to face judgment, so Christ was sacrificed once to take away the sins of many people; and he will appear a second time, not to bear sin, but to bring salvation to those who are waiting for him.

Hebrews 9:27-28

The phrase 'the second coming' does not occur in the Bible (*NIV*), but is sometimes referred to as 'the coming of the Son of Man' *(Matthew 24:27, 37, 39),* or 'the coming of our Lord Jesus Christ' *(2 Thessalonians 2:1).* There are other Scripture verses and hundreds of references regarding the time when Jesus Christ will return to this earth as the 'King of Kings' *(Revelation 19:16).*

Prophetically speaking, it is as certain and integral to the Bible's story as his first coming as a vulnerable baby born in Bethlehem. However, part of the greatest attraction of the Book of Revelation is the way in which it portrays Jesus as he is right now, in his rightful majesty and authority and in contrast to the suffering Messiah who came the first time.

The two 'comings' and the differing roles of Christ go hand in hand, but any doubt which remains regarding Jesus' sovereignty and divinity will be swept away when on his return he comes in devastating glory. For this reason perhaps the most apt biblical title given to this moment is 'the glorious appearing of our great God and Saviour, Jesus Christ' *Titus 2:13*.

Armageddon

Then they gathered the kings together to the place that in Hebrew is called Armageddon.

Revelation 16:16

'The battle of Armageddon' is not a scriptural expression, but is named after the place called the Valley of Megiddo, where Satan, his antichrist and false prophet, draw together an evil conspiracy of leaders from across the world to fight against Jesus Christ himself.

Then I saw three evil spirits that looked like frogs; they came out of the mouth of the dragon, out of the mouth of the beast and out of the mouth of the false prophet. They are spirits of demons performing miraculous signs, and they go out to the kings of the whole world, to gather them for the battle on the great day of God Almighty.

Revelation 16:13, 14

'The battle on the great day of God Almighty' is a more accurate, biblical description of this event, and it is either a very brief battle or just briefly described in Revelation 19:11-21. This underlines the arrogance of Satan, and indeed of humankind, to think they would be any sort of match against God himself.

There is no wisdom, no insight, no plan that can succeed against the LORD.

Proverbs 21:30

To reach such a hatred for Jesus that one would be willing to try and fight him, reveals the lying ability of Satan's perfect man. It also reveals the degree of hatred and jealousy the world has against the Jews, and Israel whom God protects. It may be a backlash against the anger felt if millions of Christians had been previously 'caught up' in a Rapture. It may also be a combination of all these things, along with a subconscious recognition that Christ's fearsome holiness would surely reveal an individual's sinfulness.

The Millennial Kingdom

This term refers to a period of 1,000 years, and will be used in relation to Revelation 20:1-8 which describes the scene after the Tribulation, and after the second coming of Christ.

Following the battle at Armageddon, Christ will judge the living nations and bring back to life those who became believers but then died during the seven-year Tribulation. Christ will reign with

15

them and those Christians who were still alive for a literal period of 1,000 years, while the devil will be bound, restraining his rebellion.

Following this 1,000 year period the devil will be loosed a little while (***Revelation 20:7-10***), and a final rebellion will ensue, revealing humankind's inherent sin despite having the freewill to choose Christ. This specific amount of time will be proof to us all that even with God himself ruling in our physical presence, many of us will still reject him. So much for the idea that people would believe if only they could see him!

This information may sound staggering to those who have not come across it before. This futurist interpretation of the text and ordering of events adheres to pre-millennialism – that is, a belief that Jesus Christ will return, and then rule for 1,000 years. Other interpretations exist, but they require an unnecessarily complex understanding and symbolism of the text.

The first of these other interpretations is called 'post-millennialism'. It is a belief that *after* a 1,000 year period Christ will return to rule on earth. This is usually in conjunction with a belief that either the Church will usher in his Kingdom through a 1,000 year period of worldwide acceptance of the gospel, or else the world will become a better and better place until it is ready for Christ to return and naturally be accepted by humankind.

Post-millennialism struggles as soon as one considers the state of the world and its readiness (as opposed to its need) to accept Jesus and his gospel. It also struggles to explain its unusual chronology compared to a plain reading of Scripture.

The second alternative to pre-millennialism is the denial of a literal 1,000 years, known as 'amillennialism'. This belief takes the relevant text as being symbolic, interpreting it as denoting a long period of time, and sometimes used to describe a time period in history or even in Heaven.

Pre-millennialism is the most logical view when read in the context of related eschatology. By taking the relevant Bible texts in their most simple, literal form, it is possible to receive a much more straightforward understanding of the chronology of events. Readers may make up their own minds by reading the main text for themselves, and asking whether the Millennial Kingdom appears to arrive *after* Christ's return, *before* it, or whether the Scripture indicates that it is not to be taken literally at all:

'And I saw an angel coming down out of heaven, having the key to the Abyss and holding in his hand a great chain. He seized the dragon, that ancient serpent, who is the devil, or Satan, and bound him for a thousand years. He threw him into the Abyss, and locked and sealed it over him, to keep him from deceiving the nations anymore until the thousand years were ended. After that, he must be set free for a short time.

I saw thrones on which were seated those who had been given authority to judge. And I saw the souls of those who had been beheaded because of their testimony for Jesus and because of the word of God. They had not worshiped the beast or his image and had not received his mark on their foreheads or their hands. They came to life and reigned with Christ a thousand years. (The rest of the dead did not come to life until the thousand years were ended.) This is the first resurrection. Blessed and holy are those who have part in the first resurrection. The second death has no power over them, but they will be priests of God and of Christ and will reign with him for a thousand years. When the thousand years are over, Satan will be released from his prison and will go out to deceive the nations in the four corners of the earth - Gog and Magog - to gather them for battle.'

Revelation 20:1-8

The Millennial Kingdom is alluded to many times throughout Scripture, but in this short passage it is given a specific time-frame on six occasions within just eight verses. Would this would be the case if the time-frame was just symbolic?

After the 1,000 years there is to be a final battle, with an unsurprising rebellion led by Satan and an equally unsurprising victory for Christ. After this every unbeliever will be raised to stand before the Great White Throne *(Revelation 20:11-15)*, on which Jesus sits in final and just judgment. This is the last thing to happen before we enjoy our eternity in the new Heaven, and the ultimate purpose of God's creation is finally fulfilled.

On the following pages are some elementary illustrations of the chronology involved when we put these references together on a time-scale. It is deliberately uncomplicated in order that those who are new to the subject may begin to develop a mental picture of eschatological events and how the Rapture concept proposes to be a part of them. I found such visual aids helpful when I was first introduced to such matters. So this drawing is merely offered as a memorable supporting framework for the work that follows.

There are dozens of other key themes and eschatological peculiarities that would deserve to be defined and illustrated if this were a study on biblical end-time prophecy in general. However, for the sake of brevity I have limited our references to those that will necessarily be mentioned further on in the book.These will help us in considering whether the Rapture concept is biblically valid.

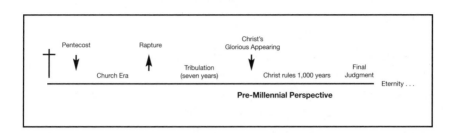

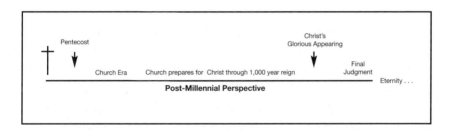

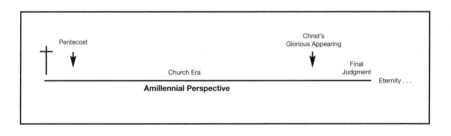

What is the next event?

The Bible has a beginning and an end. Such a simple statement is true not only in terms of its pages, but also in terms of its message.

As Genesis begins with God's Creation, so Revelation ends with the fulfilment of creation's purpose. This is clearly seen as the Bible is read through from start to finish. Even at a glance we notice some interesting comparisons between these two books which testify to their being a part of the same story, one at each end.

For example, both speak of a paradise, one that was lost, one that is to come, and within both we find the Tree of Life (cf **Genesis 3:22-24**; *Revelation 22:2*). Within these books we read of the start and the end of humankind's rebellion against God, as well as the first death *(Genesis 4:8)* and the promise that death will be no more *(Revelation 21:4).* Even the devil is first introduced *(Genesis 3:1-8)* and then finally doomed *(Revelation 20:10)* as we compare the beginning and end of this story.

The great assurance comes in the knowledge that it is *God's* story. He is the Author and nothing in it will occur outside his control, mercy, love and wisdom.

I am the Alpha and the Omega, the First and the Last, the Beginning and the End.
Revelation 22:13

In between the beginning and the end of the Bible, therefore, we have just one story, delivered through many authors, over many centuries, and with countless sub-plots. The story of the Bible is the message that God has created us with the intention of living in relationship with us, but through our inherent choice to sin we fall short of his glorious holiness, and are neither worthy nor capable of being in his presence. As the story progresses we are provided with guidelines and examples of his holy standards and our inability to maintain them. These guidelines lead to the realisation that what humankind needed was a Messiah, a Saviour, someone who would save us from the consequence of our sin, and restore our relationship with the holy Lord Almighty.

Jesus Christ, therefore, is the focal point of Scripture. Not only are we told that all things were created through him *(Colossians 1:16)*, but, having lost our purity through our sin, our Creator sacrificed himself by being cruelly killed on a cross. He did this in order to atone for our impurity, thereby giving us access to God's throne through his own pure and holy blood (for example *Hebrews 9:26-28*).

But the story did not end there. Following Jesus' death he came back to life again three days later, an assurance that those who trust in him will also conquer death. Then after his ascension back to Heaven he sent us the Holy Spirit, who guides us according to God's holy will.

The New Testament provides many wonderful letters in which the role of the Holy Spirit is described and the responsibility of the Christian is asserted. In the background there is the constant reminder that God's will is continually being accomplished, and at a time of his choosing he will bring an end to this story. Thereafter another story will begin, a story which is set in Heaven, and for which this current 'scene' has been just a preparation.

Revelation 21:1-5 helps us to envisage this new scene:
'Then I saw a new Heaven and a new earth, for the first heaven and the first earth had passed away, and there was no longer any sea. I saw the Holy City, the new Jerusalem, coming down out of heaven from God, prepared as a bride beautifully dressed for her

husband. And I heard a loud voice from the throne saying, "Now the dwelling of God is with men, and he will live with them. They will be his people, and God himself will be with them and be their God. He will wipe every tear from their eyes. There will be no more death or mourning or crying or pain, for the old order of things has passed away."

He who was seated on the throne said, "I am making everything new!"'

However, if God's story through the Bible has a beginning and an end, which introduces the everlasting 'sequel', then it is little wonder that it has often been a Christian trait to consider just at what stage in the story we are presently living in. The question is this:

How near to the end of the story is the era in which we are now alive and serving God?

In relation to this question, we must acknowledge that there are some things we can know, and some things which we simply cannot know. What we can be sure of is what has already passed, because the Bible tells us the story so far. We also know that *before* the story of the Bible *ends* and the new story begins, there are evidently still a few matters which await fulfilment. Therefore we are obviously not quite at the 'end' just yet. This is why attention is now being brought upon biblical eschatology, including the book of Revelation, despite its abuse over the centuries since it was written.

In other words the renewed interest in eschatology is not only in the search for knowledge, but also a search for understanding of our place within that 'story'.

Although the Bible is teeming with eschatological hints, declarations, and promises, the book of the Revelation of Jesus

Christ is the one which is particularly concerned with the details regarding this story's final chapter.

The previous chapter gives a brief idea of the interpretation of the book of Revelation. It is described as a prophecy that Jesus Christ is to return to the earth as surely as he came the first time. This time, he will come not as a vulnerable baby, but as the mighty King of kings to defeat those who oppose him and to ultimately usher in the heavenly Kingdom. At that point the new, yet intrinsically linked, story begins.

The above summary of the Bible omits many sub-plots, but in doing so we have also yet to list many of the events which the Bible describes as being God's way of miraculously maintaining the storyline.

Having summarised the story's basic plot, what follows is a condensed list of miraculous events throughout the Bible in which God intervened in a direct way. These may be considered as being the Author's method of ensuring that the story's momentum does not stall, while drawing attention to his omnipotence, omniscience and sovereignty. If the focal point of the Bible's story is Jesus Christ, then each of these events acts as a reminder that nothing was going to stop God from implementing his plan of salvation.

Some of these may be so well known or obvious that the awesome power and meaning behind them might become easily missed. If so, then perhaps it would help to consider each event in the context of the whole story as summarised above. God brought these events about for the sake of having an intimate relationship with us here, and in the hereafter.

Miraculous events which God has included in his story, as found in Scripture:

23

➤ The Creation of the world *Genesis 1*
➤ The great flood *Genesis 6-8*
➤ The confusion of Babel with the creation of languages *Genesis 11:1-9*
➤ The (predicted) destruction of Sodom *Genesis 19*
➤ Lot's wife being turned into a pillar of salt *Genesis 19:26*
➤ Enoch suddenly 'vanishing' *Genesis 5:24, Hebrews 11:5*
➤ Joseph's prophetic dreams and his ability to interpret others - plus God's provision for Israel through his adversity *Genesis 37-50*
➤ The flaming bush that did not burn *Exodus 3:2*
➤ Moses' rod turning into a serpent (and back again) *Exodus 4:3, 4, 30; 7:10, 12*
➤ Moses' leprous hand *Exodus 4:6, 7, 30*
➤ The 10 plagues in Egypt *Exodus 7-12,*
➤ The plague on Israel *Numbers 16:46-50*
➤ The guiding pillar of cloud and fire *Exodus 13:21, 22; 14:19, 20*
➤ The separation of the Red Sea *Exodus 14:22*
➤ The destruction of Pharaoh and his army *Exodus 14:23-30*
➤ The sweetening of the waters of Marah *Exodus 15:25*
➤ The manna sent to feed the Israelites *Exodus 16:4-31*
➤ The quail sent to feed the Israelites *Exodus 16:13*
➤ The water which came from the rock *Exodus 17:6*
➤ Balaam's donkey speaks *Numbers 22:23-30*
➤ The Jordan River is divided *Joshua 3:14-17; 4:16-18*
➤ The dew on/off Gideon's fleece *Judges 6:37-40*
➤ Fire on the sacrifice of Elijah *1 Kings 18:38*
➤ Elijah fed by ravens *1 Kings 17:6*
➤ Elijah fed by an angel *1 Kings 19:1-8*
➤ Elijah increases the widow's meal and oil *1 Kings 17:9-16;*
➤ Elijah raises the widow's son *1 Kings 17:17-24*
➤ Rain falls after drought in answer to Elijah's prayer *1 Kings 18:41-45*
➤ Elijah brings fire down upon Ahaziah's army *2 Kings 1:10-12*

- Elijah divides the Jordan River *2 Kings 2:8*
- Elijah is taken up to the heavens *2 Kings 2:11*
- Elisha divides the Jordan River *2 Kings 2:14*
- Elisha sweetens the waters of Jericho *2 Kings 2:19-22*
- Elisha increases a widow's supply of oil *2 Kings 4:1-7*
- Elisha raises the dead child *2 Kings 4:18-37*
- Elisha detoxifies the poisoned stew *2 Kings 4:38-41*
- Elisha feeds 100 men *2 Kings 4:42-44*
- Elisha cures Naaman *2 Kings 5:1-19*
- Elisha strikes down Gehazi with leprosy *2 Kings 5:26, 27*
- Elisha makes the axe-head float *2 Kings 6:6*
- Elisha enables others to see spiritual things *2 Kings 6:17*
- Elisha strikes a whole army with blindness *2 Kings 6:18*
- The bones of Elisha raise a dead man to life *2 Kings 13:21*
- Isaiah causes the shadow to retreat on the sun dial *2 Kings 20:9-11*
- Hezekiah is cured *Isaiah 38:1-5*
- Shadrach, Meshach, and Abednego survive the furnace *Daniel 3:23-28*
- Daniel survives the lions' den *Daniel 6:16-24*
- Jonah survives/saved in the belly of the great fish *Jonah 1:17-2:10*
- Jesus' fulfillment of prophecy is a bundle of miracles in itself, but also …
- The incarnation of Jesus *Matthew 1:18-25; Luke 1:26-80*
- The appearance of the star over Bethlehem *Matthew 2:1-9*
- The rescue of baby Jesus *Matthew 2:13-23*
- Jesus turns water into wine *John 2:1-11*
- Jesus heals the nobleman's son *John 4:46-54*
- Jesus predicts/instructs the catch of fish *Luke 5:1-11*
- Jesus heals the demoniac *Mark 1:23-26; Luke 4:33-36*
- Jesus heals Peter's mother-in-law *Matthew 8:14-15; Mark 1:29-31*
- Jesus cleanses the leper *Matthew 8:1-4; Mark 1:40-45*
- Jesus heals the paralysed man *Mark 2:1-12; Luke 5:17-26*

25

- Jesus heals the immobile man *John 5:1-9*
- Jesus restores the withered hand *Matthew 12:9-13*
- Jesus heals the centurion's servant *Luke 7:1-10*
- Jesus raises the widow's son to life *Luke 7:11-16*
- Jesus heals another demoniac *Matthew 12:22; Luke 11:14*
- Jesus stills the storm *Mark 4:35-41*
- Jesus throws demons out of two men *Matthew 8:28-34*
- Jesus raises Jairus' daughter from the dead *Luke 8:41-56*
- Jesus cures the woman with the issue of blood *Mark 5:25-34*
- Jesus restores sight to two blind men *Matthew 9:27-31*
- Jesus heals another demoniac *Matthew 9:32, 33*
- Jesus walks on water *Matthew 14:22-33*
- Jesus heals the daughter of the non-Jewish, Syro-Phoenician woman *Mark 7:24-30*
- Jesus feeds more than 4,000 people with little *Matthew 15:32-38*
- Jesus restores the deaf-mute man *Mark 7:31-37*
- Jesus restores sight to a blind man *Mark 8:22-26*
- Jesus heals the epileptic boy *Luke 9:37-42*
- Jesus obtains the temple tax from a fish's mouth *Matthew 17:24-27*
- Jesus heals 10 lepers *Luke 17:11-19*
- Jesus opens the eyes of a man born blind *John 9*
- Jesus raises Lazarus from the dead *John 11:1-46*
- Jesus heals a woman *Luke 13:10-13*
- Jesus cures a man with dropsy *Luke 14:1-4*
- Jesus restores sight to blind Bartimaeus *Mark 10:46-52*
- Jesus condemns a fig tree *Matthew 21:18-20*
- Jesus heals the ear of Malchus *Luke 22:49-51*
- Jesus instructs/predicts the second catch of fish *John 21:3-6*
- Jesus sends the 70 (or 72) who perform miracles *Luke 10:17-20*
- Jesus predicts his own death in type *John 3:14*
- Jesus predicts his own resurrection *Matthew 12:40; Mark 8:31; John 2:19*

- Jesus is raised from the dead *Matthew 28:7; Mark 16:6; Luke 24:34; John 20:18*
- Many dead are brought to life at once *Matthew 27:52*
- Jesus physically appears from nowhere *John 20:19-20, 26-28*
- Jesus ascends to Heaven, promising another *Luke 24:49-51; Acts 1:7-9*
- The Holy Spirit comes at Pentecost *Acts 2:1-4*

Then we have a few accounts of post-Pentecost miracles

- Peter and John cure a lame man *Acts 3:2-11*
- The death of Ananias and Sapphira *Acts 5:5-10*
- Peter cures the sick *Acts 5:15, 16*
- Peter heals Aeneas *Acts 9:33, 34*
- Peter raises Dorcas from the dead *Acts 9:36-41*
- Peter and other apostles are delivered from prison *Acts 5:17-23; 12:6-11; 16:23-30*
- Philip carried away by the Spirit *Acts 8:39*
- Paul hears God, is stricken blind and subsequently cured of blindness *Acts 9:3-18*
- Paul strikes Elymas (Bar-Jesus) with blindness *Acts 13:11*
- Paul heals a cripple *Acts 14:8-10*
- Paul throws out evil spirits, and cures sick people *Acts 16:18; 19:11, 12; 28:8, 9*
- Paul raises Eutychus to life *Acts 20:9-12*

These are 100 or so of the more obvious acts of divine intervention recorded in the Bible. There are many more which could have been listed, and between each of these there are countless further acts of God which are brought about in a more subtle manner, through circumstance, nature or the ministry of God's people.

It is clear that miraculous events are an inseparable part of the story of God and his desire to bring us into a relationship with him, which commences in this life but lasts for eternity. Some of these events are on a larger scale than others. Some come with human cooperation, some do not.

This all leads us to ask, 'What's next in the storyline?' Is the 'next event' also the 'final event', which is the return of Christ to rule? And if this is the case, then is it imminent?

In answer to the question 'What next?', attention must be drawn to four factors.

Firstly, as we scan the above list from the Bible we would be justified in saying that the last *major* event brought about by God in a miraculous, or at least spectacular and directly intervening way, was when the Holy Spirit came at Pentecost.

The arrival of the Holy Spirit in the Church was not the *original* Pentecost. It simply took place on the annual Jewish day of Pentecost. It is not coincidental that this amazing phenomenon should take place on such a day. It was certainly God's intention. It was a fulfilment of prophecy, the reasons for which we shall detail in a later chapter. I draw attention to this now to indicate that it may well be acceptable to consider whether the next *major* event has been prophesied in the same way for our benefit, and is awaiting our understanding of the relevant biblical texts.

Secondly, when considering 'What next?' we need to be aware that the second coming of Jesus Christ is not the next thing to happen in the story of the Bible. When he comes to judge between the righteous and unrighteous as 'sheep and goats' (Matthew 25:31-33) and then to reign on earth (Revelation 20:4-6) this will be the last thing prior to our eternity with him in Heaven (Revelation 21:1-4). Therefore the second coming is not imminent.

For now, this claim may be simply based on the knowledge that prior to this event the antichrist, man of sin, or man of

lawlessness has yet to make his earthly appearance
(2 Thessalonians 2:3-4). He is yet to confirm a peace treaty with
many nations (Daniel 9:27) which will subsequently be broken.
The prophesied battle at Armageddon has yet to occur (Revelation
16:16). This is based on the plainest interpretation of such texts,
and such an approach seems to make the most sense.

**Evidently, then, the Church is in for a shock if it thinks Jesus'
rule on earth is the next event.**

Thirdly, most Christians who have spent even the briefest amount
of time in considering God's prophetic timeline believe that the
'next event' involves an end of this life, and the beginning of
another – this time with a new, heavenly body and in new,
heavenly surroundings. Such a simple stance, though taking no
account of other future events that have yet to occur, is nevertheless
accurate for Christians if the Rapture idea is to be believed.

Fourthly, it is completely reasonable for the Christian who believes
in the supernatural power of God and the authority of Scripture to
be content with the notion that God's next chapter in his story
might involve something *equally* miraculous, *equally* dramatic and
equally supernatural to what he has demonstrated in the past. This
is the main reason for listing the miracle events above.

The only thing that may cause us to doubt this is that such action
has not been taken by God for a long period of time – nearly
2,000 years if we are to use the Holy Spirit's arrival as a marker.
In God's eternal perspective such a time lapse may be considered
irrelevant. If he plans to carry out something as dramatic as the
proposed Rapture, then the testimony from Scripture is that such
an act would actually be in keeping with his story so far.

To summarise: the Bible is one story – God's story – in which
there is a beginning and an end. Its end introduces the sequel, the

story of eternity. The Bible's story tells us that God wants to live in relationship with us, and has made this possible through trust in what Jesus Christ did for us. This has enabled us to enter Heaven by his grace through faith alone in his innocent blood. It is only natural to question where we are in relation to the story's ending, and it is also natural to consider what may be the *next event* as the story continues to unfold.

The end has not yet come, as the end is brought about by the second coming of Jesus Christ to rule on earth and thereafter to usher in the heavenly Kingdom. We know the end is *not* imminent because there are still other chapters of the Bible's story which have yet to be enacted. There are prophecies which have yet to be fulfilled. Nevertheless we may still consider what 'the next event' may be. By demonstrating that God has often used extremely dramatic and miraculous events and intervention in the past, it would be perfectly in keeping with his character if such a dramatic event were to occur next in his story too. All this may be summed up as follows:

The Rapture concept cannot be discounted on the grounds of being too dramatic, or too improbable. Given the story so far, in addition to what we know has yet to occur before the end, it is perfectly acceptable to consider whether this concept is biblical, and therefore whether it may be the 'next event'.

The Rapture concept

So far this book has attempted to set the eschatological scene in preparation for its main argument. It has done so:

- by outlining a rule of interpretation;
- by providing some brief definitions of key terms and themes;
- by leading the reader to the point of being open to question what may be the next major event within God's story;
- by demonstrating the need to allow for the possibility that 'the next event' may be something rather dramatic, miraculous, large-scale and evidently supernatural, in keeping both with acts of God in the past, as well as allowing for a possible Rapture in the future.

We have yet to assess the validity of the Rapture concept based purely on specific Scripture texts. That will be attempted in the following section of this book. To this point the eschatological scene has been introduced in a way that will now enable us to finally provide a description of the various Rapture concepts, fit them into our eschatological time-scale, and decide which is the most convincing idea before we study its premise in detail.

If we accept that the Bible is inspired by God, and see in it the unfolding of a divine plan, we can see that throughout history and into the future God is, and always will be, in control. While lovingly allowing for our freewill and freedom of choice, God has demonstrated that he can involve himself with his creation as and when he sees fit.

Some people may explain biblical stories of God's miraculous dealings with humankind in terms of scientific phenomena which might naturally, if improbably, occur. Others take a more literal view of such Scripture accounts, contending that God could use both the truly supernatural and the natural to fulfil his will.

The interpretation of **Exodus 7-12**, which describes the 10 plagues which God sent on Egypt , is a good example of a biblical account of divine intervention which can be understood either as a set of supernatural miracles or as a series of highly improbable, yet possible, natural phenomena which God brought about with perfect timing.

This is a simple example of the way in which God can interact with us. It demonstrates how what some might describe as being 'beyond' the natural, might be described by others as being a 'manipulation of' the natural.

This is important because whether we believe that God can and does perform truly miraculous events such as those found in the Bible may determine whether we believe in the possibility of a literal Rapture. This is because the Rapture concept is one which relies completely on direct intervention by God in a way that is beyond the known laws of nature. Scientifically speaking, I guess there is no possibility of there ever being a Rapture. Biblically speaking, however, if we believe that God supernaturally brought about the miracles which were listed in an earlier chapter, then there is good reason to believe that he may do so again through a similarly amazing event such as a Rapture, if that is what Scripture teaches.

Therefore, in describing what the Rapture concept is, we will begin with two of its key Scripture texts. We will follow this up with examples of similar phenomena which have occurred in the past, thereby demonstrating that the concept is, at the least, a proven possibility. Then we shall consider the three main differences of opinion which occur within the Rapture theory.

Rapture? ... What Rapture?

Listen, I tell you a mystery: We will not all sleep, but we will all be changed – in a flash, in the twinkling of an eye, at the last trumpet.

For the trumpet will sound, the dead will be raised imperishable,
and we will be changed. For the perishable must clothe itself with
the imperishable, and the mortal with immortality.

1 Corinthians 15:51-53

Earlier in this book we described the Rapture concept as the belief
that there will be a future event, biblically prophesied, in which
God will take Christians to be with him in Heaven. Believers who
have died will be taken first, immediately followed by those still
alive. One key text upon which the Rapture is based includes
these words *'We will not all sleep, but we will all be changed'*
*(**1 Corinthians 15:51**)*. Those who believe in the Rapture take this
to mean that not all Christians will experience physical death, but
all Christians, both the dead and those alive at this occurrence,
will be given new, imperishable and heavenly bodies. This event
is separate from the Second Coming of Jesus Christ. The Rapture
involves Christians being taken from earth to be with Christ, the
Second Coming involves Christ coming back to rule on earth.

In the very first pages of this book we also read the following
Concise Oxford Dictionary definition:

Rapture*: noun. (esp. theol.) act of transporting a person from one*
place to another (esp. heaven).

When these descriptions are combined we can more readily
understand another key text from which the Rapture concept is
derived, and after which it is named.
For the Lord himself will come down from heaven, with a loud
command, with the voice of the archangel and with the trumpet
call of God, and the dead in Christ will rise first. After that, we
who are still alive and are left will be caught up together with them
in the clouds to meet the Lord in the air. And so we will be with
the Lord forever. Therefore encourage each other with these words.

1 Thessalonians 4:16-18

The Rapture concept is based on the belief that one day Christians, first the dead and then the living, will be 'caught up', or 'transported', 'raptured' or 'translated', to be with Jesus Christ **prior** to his glorious appearing, which has become known as the Second Coming.

The word itself, 'Rapture', comes from the Latin translation of the term to be 'caught up'. The history of the concept and how it developed is a subject which belongs to a wider study, and continues to be the topic of much debate. Ultimately any Christian doctrine must be based squarely on the premise of what the Bible teaches, and that Church tradition, though useful, is secondary to biblical authority. Therefore, any doctrinal acceptance of the Rapture must ultimately be based purely on what the Bible teaches.

At the same time, while the Rapture is often considered to be defined by the Bible itself as a 'mystery' (for example **1 Corinthians 1:51**), great care needs to be taken in making sure Scripture is not being in any way abused, manipulated or taken out of context in order to construct a doctrine that is not scripturally based. Therefore while this section has provided a further definition and premise for the Rapture concept, its biblical validity will be weighed more completely and tested more vigorously in the following chapters. In seeking to establish the truth for themselves, readers should ensure that all Scripture references within this book are read in full and considered in their full context.

Where are the dead?

This is a question which really needs a separate study to answer, and is certainly too complex to answer sufficiently as a mere subsection of this book. However, it is nevertheless quite probable

that some readers, having come across the subject and de
of the Rapture for the first time, may question where the
Christ' are now, if they have yet to be resurrected to thei
eternal home.

Therefore it is appropriate to answer such a question by
highlighting the fact that wherever they are, we know that they
are not in their *final* heavenly home.

It could well be that they are in a form of paradise (*Luke 23:43*),
yet awaiting the resurrection which will provide them with their
new, imperishable bodies (*1 Corinthians 15:52-54*). It could well
be that those who have not accepted Christ are equally aware of
their status (*Luke 16:19-31*). We know that it would certainly be
in keeping with biblical resurrection theology for 'sleeping'
believers to be safe and at peace with other believers until the day
of resurrection. This day is to be announced by that 'last trumpet',
when we know the dead in Christ will be raised. This will be just
before the living are caught up in the Rapture, at which point
there will be the most amazing reunion (*1 Thessalonians
4:13-18*).

Jesus himself silenced those who doubted the resurrection with
sound logic, but only after referring to it as something which has
yet to occur (*Mark 12:18-27*). When added to the apostle Paul's
teaching we can have no doubt that the resurrection was a much
anticipated future event, at which time we shall all go to Heaven
together.

The Rapture plausibility

Having provided two of the key texts upon which the Rapture
concept is based, along with a couple of definitions to help
introduce what it is in its most simple form, it would be helpful at

this stage to provide a few 'reminders' as to the plausibility of this belief.

The first 'reminder' is the fact that there are key biblical texts which proponents of the concept believe prophesy and teach a future Rapture. A couple of these have been mentioned, and many more will follow.

The second 'reminder' was more fully explained in an earlier chapter when we outlined a list of 100 or so miraculous events within Scripture which were a part of God's story. They served as an example that God has no problem with using supernatural means to accomplish his eternal plan. The Rapture, therefore, is possible in that, if scripturally valid, it would generally be in keeping with some of the direct ways in which God has intervened throughout history.

Thirdly, we can actually see within the Bible's pages some more specific examples of God's intervention which are 'Rapture-like'. In other words, there have been occasions in God's story when he has been the author of events which have striking similarities to the Rapture concept as defined above. There may be others but the examples of Enoch, Elijah, post-resurrection Jesus, Philip, the Transfiguration, and of angels will suffice.

Enoch
Enoch walked with God; then he was no more, because God took him away.

Genesis 5:24

By faith Enoch was taken from this life, so that he did not experience death; he could not be found, because God had taken him away. For before he was taken, he was commended as one who pleased God.

Hebrew 11:5

These Bible verses may be interpreted in various ways, but if read plainly it really does appear as if Enoch was 'caught up' in exactly the same way that the Rapture concept proposes. If so, then not only would the Rapture have a precedent, but this would add weight to the argument that God may do the same again.

It is also worth noticing the type of man Enoch was: *'one who pleased God'* and *'walked with God'*. Perhaps this would have a bearing when considering who will be taken in a Rapture, and what sort of lives they should be striving to live in the meantime.

Elijah

As they were walking along and talking together, suddenly a chariot of fire and horses of fire appeared and separated the two of them, and Elijah went up to Heaven in a whirlwind.

2 Kings 2:11

This is another occurrence of a Rapture-like event. It was one that Elijah had expected to happen, (though he didn't know the exact timing), and one which the prophets at the time were foretelling (*2 Kings 2:3, 5, 10*). It is worth noting that he was simply walking along talking to another when he was suddenly 'caught up' to Heaven.

Should we interpret these verses Rapture-like literally? If we do not do so we must find an unnecessarily complicated rationale as to what really happened.

Jesus Christ

After he said this, he was taken up before their very eyes, and a cloud hid him from their sight.
They were looking intently up into the sky as he was going, when suddenly two men dressed in white stood beside them. 'Men of Galilee,' they said, 'why do you stand here looking into the sky?

This same Jesus, who has been taken from you into heaven, will come back in the same way you have seen him go into Heaven.'

Acts 1:9-11

Jesus Christ's ascension provides yet another Rapture-like event, adding to the plausibility of a future Rapture. On this occasion the Rapture was witnessed, along with the promise that he would return. If Jesus was *'taken up before their very eyes'* then it is clear that, should it be within his will, all Christians may likewise be 'taken up' or 'caught up' at his call.

However, Jesus' evidence for the Rapture's plausibility does not start and end with his ascension. There were many occasions when he 'appeared' to his disciples after his resurrection, and his appearances always seemed to have a sudden, unexpected or supernatural element to them. In addition to this, Scripture indicates that the majority of post-resurrection appearances occurred after he had returned to Heaven.

Jesus said, 'Do not hold on to me, for I have not yet returned to the Father. Go instead to my brothers and tell them, "I am returning to my Father and your Father, to my God and your God." '

John 20:17

Afterward Jesus appeared in a different form to two of them while they were walking in the country.

Mark 16:12

One might question what is meant by appearing in a 'different form'. We may speculate that he was now in his immortal, imperishable body, but that this body was still physical is evidenced by a further miraculous 'appearing'.

A week later his disciples were in the house again, and Thomas was with them. Though the doors were locked, Jesus came and

stood among them and said, 'Peace be with you!' Then he said to
Thomas, 'Put your finger here; see my hands. Reach out your hand
and put it into my side. Stop doubting and believe.'

John 20:26-27

'*Though the doors were locked*' is a clear indication that Jesus had
managed to simply appear among them, and yet he was in a
physical body, this was not just a spirit or ghost, for he could be
touched.

Each of these post-resurrection appearances may be understood as
being further proof that the possibility of a future Rapture is
something which is in keeping with the way God works. **Whether
we are on earth or in Heaven seems to be purely a matter of his
will**. We might take this further to assume that if we are here by
his will, then we are here for a purpose too, with all the positive
spiritual understanding we can reason from that.

On the matter of the possibility of there being a future Rapture,
then, the many post-resurrection appearances and disappearances
of Jesus in a physical body indicates that our limited
understanding of time, matter and space are exactly that – limited!

Philip

The apostle Philip was no stranger to great signs and miracles,
and God often enabled him to use such within his ministry (for
example *Acts 8:6, 13*). We may wonder what happened when
Philip had finished speaking with the newly converted Eunuch,
and was suddenly 'taken away' by the Spirit of the Lord, only to
'appear' elsewhere.

*Then both Philip and the eunuch went down into the water and
Philip baptised him. When they came up out of the water, the
Spirit of the Lord suddenly took Philip away, and the eunuch did
not see him again, but went on his way rejoicing. Philip, however,*

appeared at Azotus and traveled about, preaching the gospel in all the towns until he reached Caesarea.

Acts 8:38-40

This piece of evidence is in no way conclusive, but it is still worth noting in case it adds to the possibility that even after Jesus' ascension God may have continued to use Rapture-like events as and when he saw fit.

However, there are two last factors which, though many more may exist, are worth a special mention with regard to the possibility of a future Rapture.

The Transfiguration

The Transfiguration and the frequent stories of angels appearing are slightly different events to those listed above in that the 'Rapture' is reversed. In the Transfiguration (***Matthew 17:1***) we get to see that Elijah, who had previously been taken up to Heaven, returns to speak with Jesus about his impending death, along with Moses (***Luke 9:30, 31***). Peter witnessed the event. Though he stumbles in his thinking by offering to construct a shelter for each of them, he is obviously convinced enough by their presence to suggest that both these Old Testament characters may require shelters. If it were a mere vision then one could contend that Peter would not have made such an offer to these who were *standing* on top of a mountain.

Of course, it is clear that if God can take people up to Heaven at will, then he can send them back too, and we have already seen that this is what Jesus did frequently after his resurrection. Perhaps what is even more important is the *way* in which Jesus was transfigured. One minute he is bound in an earthly body, the next minute he is glowing as if he is back in Heaven.

After six days Jesus took Peter, James and John with him and led them up a high mountain, where they were all alone. There he was

transfigured before them. His clothes became dazzling white, whiter
than anyone in the world could bleach them. And there appeared
before them Elijah and Moses, who were talking with Jesus.
Peter said to Jesus, 'Rabbi, it is good for us to be here. Let us put
up three shelters – one for you, one for Moses and one for Elijah.'
(He did not know what to say, they were so frightened.)
Then a cloud appeared and enveloped them, and a voice came
from the cloud: 'This is my Son, whom I love. Listen to him!'
Suddenly, when they looked around, they no longer saw anyone
with them except Jesus.

Mark 9:2-8

So God's story reveals a series of Rapture-like events taking people
from the earth according to his will and timing. It also reveals a
reverse-Rapture in the form of appearances on earth from those
who God wishes to send back. In both cases the Bible certainly
does offer strong support to the future Rapture concept. Even
before we get to the most persuasive pieces of biblical evidence
for the Rapture we have already seen that not only is God a
miracle-worker, but he has used various Rapture-like methods in
the past. These add more weight to the idea that he is planning to
do it again in the future.

The angels
Finally we come to the abundant accounts throughout the entire
Bible of angels appearing and disappearing again between the very
presence of God in Heaven and various places here on earth. They
come with messages of all kinds, and their stories are simply too
numerous to list here, as a glimpse at a concordance will confirm.

The point is that one may suggest that each and every appearance
of an angel is in itself a form of Rapture, whether it is in their
appearing or their disappearing back to Heaven again. For each
'journey' the plausibility of a future Rapture is enhanced. When
we consider that it was not unusual for the angels to take on

human form (for example *Genesis 18:19*), and that there will have been many other, unrecorded angelic visits too (for example *Hebrews 13:2*) we are given another reminder that the probability of God ever incorporating a Rapture-like event in the future is higher than one might first imagine.

The Rapture, then, is far more plausible than one might initially believe if one takes into account these three things: what the Bible specifically teaches regarding a future Rapture, the supernatural methods which God has generously used in order to accomplish his story, and the many Rapture-like events which have occurred in the past.

However, for the Rapture concept to be persuasive and biblically valid as a future event, the specific teaching from Scripture needs to be given more weight.

The Rapture's timing …

When it comes to matters of eschatology it is essential to be aware of the chronology of events. At the same time it is even more important to be aware of what is biblically prophesied and what is mere conjecture. We must also recognise that there are some elements with regard to timing which should not even be open to such conjecture.

So let us start by making a simple statement around which an idea of timing can be based. With regard to the Rapture's timing, differences of opinion tend to relate to where the event occurs in relation to the Tribulation period.

Here is a brief summary of what this time of Tribulation is:
- At some point in the future, according to a futurist interpretation, there will be a seven-year covenant confirmed

by the 'ruler to come' and involving the Jewish people which he will break midway (**Daniel 9:27**), revealing his deception.

This will spark off a realisation by many people that Jesus really was and is the Messiah. There will be both a terrible persecution by the 'beast' (**Revelation 13:5-9**), as well as a tremendous time of evangelisation by the new Messianic Jews (**Revelation 7:4-14**).

- We do not know when this initial covenant will be signed, nor do we know the identity of the ruler who will confirm it.
- These same seven years are the remaining seven of Daniel's 70 'weeks' of years which were appointed to God's people of Israel (**Daniel 9:24**), and they will include God's wrath designed to shake securities and encourage a choice to be made between Christ and antichrist (for example **Revelation 11:13**).
- Because of the trials, persecution and trouble during this time it is known as the Tribulation, and sometimes the second half is called the 'Great Distress' (**Matthew 24:15-21**).
- The seven years will end with the glorious appearing of Jesus Christ at his Second Coming, as he defeats the antichrist's armies at Armageddon (**Revelation 19:11-21**) and reigns for 1,000 years (**Revelation 20:4-6**).
- Then he will reveal the new Heaven on earth in which we shall live for eternity (**Revelation 21**).

In relation to this, the Rapture concept has three main opinions with regard to its timing. Either the Rapture occurs at the end of the Tribulation, in the middle of it, or precedes it. The differing views are known as the post-Tribulation, mid-Tribulation, and pre-Tribulation views respectively. These views are illustrated on the next page.

These differences of opinion are all based on the Bible, they are all sincere, and they are all matters of biblical interpretation. They agree that the Rapture concept is biblically valid, but in their respective studies they have reached different conclusions as to when the Rapture would occur and why.

Certainly, if one could travel back in time it would be interesting to see whether the same divergence occurred over the prophecies regarding Christ's first coming as the suffering Messiah. The results after that event show that a difference of opinion existed. Such variation does not mean that Christ did not come the first time, and neither does variation on the future Rapture concept indicate that it will not occur.

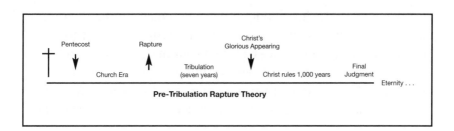

Pre-Tribulation Rapture Theory

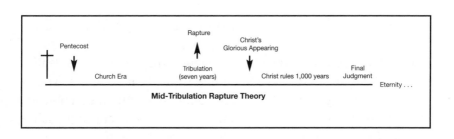

Mid-Tribulation Rapture Theory

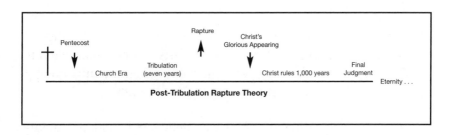

Post-Tribulation Rapture Theory

It is vital that all views on the Rapture concept are treated with respect, as they are received from fellow Christians whom we shall be greeting in eternity.

Having said that, clearly not all these variances in the theory can be true. So the remainder of this chapter will endeavour to outline what the differences are between the post, mid, and pre-Tribulation views. This will be followed by reasons for believing that one is more sustainable than the others. We will also look at some of the traditional objections to this viewpoint.

The post-Tribulation Rapture concept

As the name suggests, this asserts that the Church (that is, all people who have made a personal decision to acknowledge their sin and accept God's free gift of salvation through Christ's death and resurrection) will have to endure God's time of wrath. This is because the Rapture will not occur until Israel's final seven years have been completed. This Rapture would then occur immediately before Christ's Second Coming, his glorious appearing. So Christians would be taken up and return to earth almost in one movement.

People who take this view argue that any other timing for the Rapture equates to three 'comings' of Christ, rather than two, and that this view sits particularly comfortably when the millennial kingdom of **Revelation 20:1-8** is not taken literally.

Opponents of this view question why believers would be 'caught up' only to be immediately brought back to reign on earth again. They also raise scriptural objections to the suggestion that the Church will not escape God's wrath. (We will look at this idea later.) Further difficulties occur when considering the glaring absence of the Church within Scripture passages which deal with the Tribulation. This view does not teach an imminent return of

Christ for his bride, which is the Church (**Ephesians 5:23-32, Revelation 19:7-9**). Instead it would encourage believers to keep watch for the initial confirmation of the seven-year covenant and the antichrist.

The mid-Tribulation Rapture concept

This variation appears at first sight to be more credible than the previous one. It describes a Rapture in the middle of the seven-year Tribulation period. The Rapture would occur when the antichrist breaks his covenant and reveals his true nature. This thinking provides a logical reason why the Church would be taken out of the following half of this period. It also provides a time of 42 months during which Christ will have his bride with him in Heaven, able to celebrate the 'wedding supper' (**Revelation 19:9**) prior to returning at his Glorious Appearing.

To put it simply, for the first 42 months of the seven-year Tribulation, the Church will be on earth, but once the 'lawless one' breaks the covenant with Israel and sets up an abomination at the Jewish Temple site (**Daniel 9:27; Matthew 24:15**), then the bride of Christ will be 'taken'. Jesus Christ's glorious appearing will then occur a further 42 months later, at the end of the seven years.

Those who accept this view emphasise the Rapture-like event which takes up the 'two witnesses' in **Revelation 11:12:**

Then they heard a loud voice from Heaven saying to them, 'Come up here.' And they went up to Heaven in a cloud, while their enemies looked on.

These two are only directly identified as *the two olive trees and the two lampstands that stand before the Lord of the earth'* (**Revelation 11:4**) and so their mission and meaning during the Tribulation would need to be part of a wider study.

Mid-Tribulation Rapture proponents refer to this scenario to suggest that these figures represent Christians and Old Testament saints, who will be 'caught up' at this midway point. There is further evidence for this theory in that the final trumpet judgment of **Revelation 11:15** comes shortly after this event, and may refer to the trumpet calls found within key Rapture texts such as **1 Corinthians 15:52** and **1 Thessalonians 4:16** as previously quoted.

The mid-Tribulation Rapture concept therefore may be made to sound rather persuasive, until one takes account of several conflicting factors.

First of all, opponents of this view point out that the trumpet call of **Revelation 11:15** takes place *after* the Rapture-like event of the two witnesses, whereas the key Rapture texts place the trumpet call immediately *before* believers are 'caught up'.

Secondly they consider the two witnesses as being individuals, rather than symbols. Their characteristics, teaching, physical death and subsequent 'Rapture' all indicate that they are real people and not merely symbolic. They are referred to as 'men' (**Revelation 11:6**). In addition to which, if they represented both the Church and the Old Testament saints, and are both dead, indeed killed (**Revelation 11:7**) prior to their resurrection and rapture, then one has an impossible task of explaining the key Rapture texts that assure us that *'we will not all sleep'* (for example **1 Corinthians 15:51**).

Already, then, the mid-Tribulation Rapture concept has an unstable main premise. Both the arguments using the Rapture of the two witnesses and the seventh trumpet of Revelation 11 are insecure.

The third and final response to the mid-Tribulation Rapture concept is to return to the issue of imminence. If this theory is supported then one must also support the theory that one can foretell when the Rapture will take place. By identifying the start of the covenant, marking the beginning of the seven-years, we can know that the midway point when the covenant is broken will be exactly 42 months later. Thus we can know exactly when Christ will return for his Church.

Once again, then, we find that by adhering to this view of the Rapture's timing we also need to accept that the 'next event', or the next thing which we are to keep watch for, is not the Rapture, not the return of Jesus, but the rise of the antichrist and his covenant-making abilities.

The pre-Tribulation Rapture concept

This proposes that Jesus Christ will come to 'take up' all believers, dead and alive, to be with him in Heaven, *before* the Tribulation begins. This may be immediately before it begins, or it may be months or years before the antichrist may rise to power. Through this view we have no idea of the precise timing of the Rapture except for the indications given through world conditions, which are changeable.

Neither the post-Tribulation nor mid-Tribulation Rapture concepts teach that the Church today has much to look forward to, at least until it has endured a time of great distress. They necessarily teach that the Church is having to look toward the rise of the antichrist and his rule before being 'caught up' to be with Christ forever. These ideas do have attractive arguments for their existence, but, as we have seen, these arguments and others besides are neither persuasive nor beyond debate.

The same may be said for the pre-Tribulation Rapture concept, but this is the one which is strongest in terms of its biblical validity.

Whether it is strong enough to be able to declare that the Rapture theory is scripturally valid is the overall aim of this book, and the specific aim of the following chapters. It is chiefly because of the eschatological issue of the Rapture's imminence that the following chapters will pursue the biblical validity of the Rapture by considering the pre-Tribulation view.

This is the only view which would have the Christian keeping watch for Jesus' return for his bride, the Church, as 'the next event'. It keeps our focus on him rather than on suspect antichrists. In addition, the pre-Tribulation view of the Rapture is the only one that discourages any ideas of date-setting, or of being able to predict when the Rapture would take place. Scripture clearly indicates that such things are unknowable. The other viewpoints not only fail to observe the importance of this belief in imminence, but the arguments which they *do* propose are weaker than those of the Pre-Tribulation view.

'Therefore keep watch, because you do not know on what day your Lord will come.'

Matthew 24:42

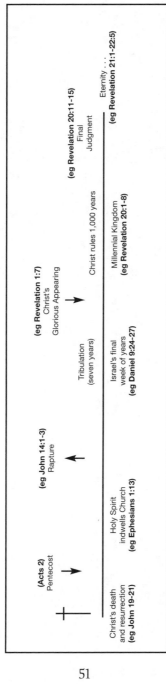

Christ's death
and resurrection
(eg John 19-21)

Holy Spirit
indwells Church
(eg Ephesians 1:13)

(Acts 2)
Pentecost

(eg John 14:1-3)
Rapture

Tribulation
(seven years)

Israel's final
week of years
(eg Daniel 9:24-27)

(eg Revelation 1:7)
Christ's
Glorious Appearing

Christ rules 1,000 years

Millennial Kingdom
(eg Revelation 20:1-8)

(eg Revelation 20:11-15)
Final
Judgment

Eternity . . .
(eg Revelation 21:1-22:5)

The Rapture and the Bible

Here is a summary of the previous section of the book.

The eschatological scene has been set by outlining some necessary definitions and preliminary considerations on end-time terms and themes.

Some of the major events and themes within eschatology were described in order to be able to better understand their relation to the Rapture.

This provided an opportunity to digest what may otherwise be difficult, and even intimidating passages and concepts regarding end-time terminology.

We placed the whole idea of a Rapture within the context of the Bible as a whole, a book containing God's story with all the wondrous and miraculous ways in which he has maintained the storyline. It was proposed that the Rapture would not be out of place as a 'next event' within such a story.

We considered the Rapture by defining what the Rapture is. We provided its key Scripture texts, and demonstrated that, biblically speaking, it is an entirely plausible concept. It was seen to be worthy of consideration as an event that could occur in the future, just as it has already occurred on occasions in the past, albeit on a smaller scale.

We outlined the three major differences held between sincere Bible-believing scholars who disagree on the timing of the

Rapture in relation to the 70th 'week' of Daniel (**Daniel 9:24-27**), also known as 'the time of wrath' (**Daniel 8:19**) or the 'Tribulation' (**Revelation 7:14**).

We have shown some of the arguments for and against the post-Tribulation and mid-Tribulation Rapture concepts, leaving what I consider to be the most convincing theory, that of a pre-Tribulation Rapture, to be examined in detail within the next three chapters.

What now follows is the biblical rationale for a pre-Tribulation Rapture concept presented in greater detail. These chapters consist of presenting a New Testament rationale, followed by an Old Testament rationale, and then offering a few more biblical considerations along with answering some objections. All this will lead to a conclusion as to whether the pre-Tribulation Rapture concept is scripturally valid.

A New Testament rationale

We have seen the history of God unfold through his Word and recognised God's plan and eternal perspective throughout its pages. Therefore it is not unreasonable to think about the future within the prophetic timescale and to consider what may be the next biblical 'event'.

This New Testament rationale starts by referring back to two of the key texts for the Rapture.

Listen, I tell you a mystery: We will not all sleep, but we will all be changed — in a flash, in the twinkling of an eye, at the last trumpet. For the trumpet will sound, the dead will be raised imperishable, and we will be changed. For the perishable must clothe itself with the imperishable, and the mortal with immortality.
1 Corinthians 15:51-53

For the Lord himself will come down from Heaven, with a loud command, with the voice of the archangel and with the trumpet call of God, and the dead in Christ will rise first. After that, we who are still alive and are left will be caught up together with them in the clouds to meet the Lord in the air. And so we will be with the Lord forever. Therefore encourage each other with these words.

1 Thessalonians 4:16-18

From these key texts, we have established that the concept of the Rapture is based on the doctrine that at some point in the future there will be a biblically prophesied event when God will take Christians to be with him in Heaven. Believers who have died will be taken first, immediately followed by those still alive.

People who believe in the Rapture say that not all Christians will experience physical death, but all Christians, both the dead and those alive at this occurrence, will be given new, imperishable and heavenly bodies. How swiftly believers are 'taken up' is not specified. While some might use previous Rapture-like events in Scripture to suggest it will be gradual enough for there to be witnesses, others would disagree. Yet all are agreed that the speed with which believers are given new imperishable bodies at the Rapture is within '*the twinkling of an eye*', or '*in a flash*'.

The idea of the Rapture is based on the belief that one day Christians, first the dead and then the living, will be 'caught up' or 'taken' to be with Jesus Christ *prior* to his glorious appearing, which has become known as the Second Coming.

The idea of the Rapture may be plausible on two counts then, firstly on the basis of its key Scripture texts, and secondly on the premise that Rapture-like events have occurred previously. The remainder of this chapter will proceed on the understanding that a future Rapture as described above is certainly plausible. It will address the specific challenge of providing further biblical evidence, including indications as to its timing in relation to Daniel's 70th week of years, according to a pre-Tribulation viewpoint. This New Testament evidence will consist of the primary things which *Jesus said*, and which *Paul wrote*, about the topic.

Things Jesus said:

'Do not let your hearts be troubled. Trust in God; trust also in me. In my Father's house are many rooms; if it were not so, I would have told you. I am going there to prepare a place for you. And if I go and prepare a place for you, I will come back and take you to be with me that you also may be where I am. You know the way to the place where I am going.'

John 14:1-4

When considering the things Jesus said regarding his return for the Church, this passage is a good place to start because of its simplicity in interpretation. It substantiates the Rapture idea in three clear ways. Firstly he told us that he was going to his *'Father's house ... to prepare a place'* for us, implying that believers have a place waiting for them in Heaven. Secondly, he said that he would come back and *'take'* us, as opposed to come and 'join' us, and thirdly he qualified this by stating that we also would be where *he* is, as opposed to him being where *we* are.

The whole tone and plainest understanding of this passage in its context is that Christ is literally preparing a place in Heaven, where he now is, and one day will come and take us there too. Quite simply, what Jesus said on this occasion is most satisfactorily explained in terms of a pre-Tribulation Rapture.

The pre-Tribulation viewpoint asserts that the Rapture is not only different from the Second Coming, which follows the reign of the antichrist, but that it precedes the seven-year covenant confirmed by the 'ruler to come', and precedes God's wrath upon the earth as detailed in **Revelation 6-19**. Indeed, it truly is the only viewpoint that maintains that Jesus Christ could come for his Church literally at any moment. According to this viewpoint every other end-time prophecy is to be fulfilled after the confirmation of the seven-year covenant, and therefore *after* the Rapture. This makes the Rapture's timing not only imminent, but also unknowable.

'No one knows about that day or hour, not even the angels in Heaven, nor the Son, but only the Father. As it was in the days of Noah, so it will be at the coming of the Son of Man. For in the days before the flood, people were eating and drinking, marrying and giving in marriage, up to the day Noah entered the ark; and they knew nothing about what would happen until the flood came and took them all away. That is how it will be at the coming of the Son of Man. Two men will be in the field; one will be taken and the other left. Two women will be grinding with a hand mill; one will be taken and the other left.
'Therefore keep watch, because you do not know on what day your Lord will come.'

Matthew 24:36-42

It is evident from Jesus' words in the above passage that we shall be living our usual, everyday lives when the Rapture occurs. *'Two men will be in the field; one will be taken and the other left. Two women will be grinding with a hand mill; one will be taken and the other left.'*

His prophecy clearly implies that we will not be hiding from persecution from a future ruler, nor suffering under the strains of global war such as Armageddon, nor concerned about various elements of wrath which God will eventually pour onto the earth. We will not have deserted our jobs in the knowledge that Christ's return for us would be within the next 42 months or seven years.

Instead, life will be continuing as normal when we are gathered to Christ.

He said to them: 'It is not for you to know the times or dates the Father has set by his own authority.'

Acts 1:7

'Therefore keep watch, because you do not know the day or the hour.'

Matthew 25:13

'No one knows about that day or hour, not even the angels in Heaven, nor the Son, but only the Father. Be on guard! Be alert! You do not know when that time will come. It's like a man going away: He leaves his house and puts his servants in charge, each with his assigned task, and tells the one at the door to keep watch. 'Therefore keep watch because you do not know when the owner of the house will come back—whether in the evening, or at midnight, or when the rooster crows, or at dawn. If he comes suddenly, do not let him find you sleeping. What I say to you, I say to everyone: "Watch!"'

Mark 13:32-37

We do not know when Christ will come for his Church. Among many other interesting and helpful things from these passages, it is worth noting that we are *not* told to 'Wait!' but to 'Watch!' This is a reminder in itself that the timing is imminent, and that the role of the Church collectively and individually is to be prepared, not 'sleeping' but 'watching'. This is in contrast to having the mid- or post-Tribulation luxury of believing that Christ will not return until midway through, or after the seven-year Tribulation, which would present the Church with a signal to 'wait', and allow it time to 'sleep'.

In addition, it is very relevant to note that we are to watch for the return of the master or house owner that is Christ. This is in contrast to 'keeping watch' for the antichrist or the confirmation of a seven-year covenant. The goal for the Church is to keep watch for Christ. Our focus should therefore be on Christ. We are told to be ready and prepared for his return, because it could literally be at any time.

From these examples from Jesus' lips it is made absolutely clear to us that we do not know when Jesus will come to take the Church. The pre-Tribulation Rapture concept is the only one which is completely in accord with this doctrine.

There are many more things which Jesus is recorded as saying on the topic of the end-times, but are not Rapture-specific. Although we shall shortly consider one final Rapture-relevant quote from Christ, it is vital to realise that on many occasions Jesus' teaching on eschatology also touched on the Tribulation, and on his Glorious Appearing. Indeed, some of the most common objections to the pre-Tribulation Rapture concept arise through disagreement from these texts as to whether Jesus was talking about the Rapture, or about his second coming to judge all nations, and how to separate them. On the above texts there can be little dispute.

Therefore, by examining the biblical evidence provided through *the things which Jesus said* on the matter of his coming for the Church, we can say that the most logical and scripturally valid Rapture theory is that which teaches the coming of the Lord Jesus Christ to take up his Church *before* the seven years of Tribulation begins. This, in turn, makes it imminent, unpredictable, and the 'next event'.

Things which Paul wrote

Jesus' words on the subject of signs of the end-times, his Glorious Appearing and the Rapture, often came in response to questions which were asked of him. Similarly, throughout Paul's letters we can piece together parts of written correspondence which either have the aim of instigating such discussion or, more frequently, were written in response to questions about the end-time.

One of our key texts is a good example of this. Both of Paul's letters to the Thessalonians seem to be the best written responses to end-time questions within the New Testament.

Brothers, we do not want you to be ignorant about those who fall asleep, or to grieve like the rest of men, who have no hope. We believe that Jesus died and rose again and so we believe that God will bring with Jesus those who have fallen asleep in him. According to the Lord's own word, we tell you that we who are still alive, who are left till the coming of the Lord, will certainly not precede those who have fallen asleep. For the Lord himself will come down from Heaven, with a loud command, with the voice of the archangel and with the trumpet call of God, and the dead in Christ will rise first. After that, we who are still alive and are left will be caught up together with them in the clouds to meet the Lord in the air. And so we will be with the Lord forever. Therefore encourage each other with these words.

1 Thessalonians 4:13-18

Both the beginning and end of the passage imply that Paul was writing these words in response to concerns his readers had regarding those believers who had died, and how their new Christ-centred theology explained their future reunion. Paul was not telling them *not* to grieve, but he was explaining that the grief Christians have for fellow Christians who had died should be different in that it contains hope, as found in the Rapture. Therefore this teaching on the Rapture seems to have arrived indirectly, as a response to a circumstance rather than as deliberate teaching on the matter.

60

This can be taken to mean several things. This could mean that Paul never saw the Rapture as being a particularly important subject which needed intentional teaching. Alternatively it could mean that Paul himself was unsure of the subject and tended to stay clear of it. But it could also mean that Paul had already provided teaching on this subject during his time with this church. Therefore he did not need to get into details or to write an exposition on the Rapture, but merely aimed to send a reminder of what he thought his readers should already know.

This third option seems to me the most likely. If his readers were only just hearing for the very first time about being *'caught up'* into the clouds then surely this passage of 'comfort' would raise far more questions than it answered. It seems more likely that Paul had previously provided at least some basic eschatological teaching so that these words were not trying to summarise the Rapture theory in just seven sentences to an audience who had never heard of it before.

In addition, it is vital to note that Paul reminds them that this teaching is *'According to the Lord's own word'.* Paul was quoting what Jesus himself had said on the matter. This is a reminder to us that Paul, and others, may certainly have learnt far more about the sequence of eschatological events than they, in turn, have passed on to us through recorded Scripture.

It is perfectly conceivable that not everything Jesus said on the matter, nor everything that Paul or other apostles taught about the Rapture, is contained within our Bible. This is not to make claims that extra-biblical teaching holds equal authority to Scripture. That would be highly dangerous, especially after 2,000 years. It is suggesting that the New Testament rationale for the Rapture is solely based on what is recorded in its pages.

We have, through the Bible, jigsaw pieces which give us a fairly good picture of the Rapture. When piecing them together it helps us to remember that they are just portions of what Jesus taught on the matter, or just written responses by Paul and other New Testament writers. Christ and the New Testament authors had the whole picture, but we have only some pieces which we glean from Scripture.

The relevance of this approach is obvious. Firstly, just because we do not have a comprehensive scriptural description of all that the Rapture entails does not mean it is not valid. Secondly, the existence of various jigsaw pieces relating to the Rapture proves that there *is* a whole picture waiting to be rediscovered. So, thirdly, we can look for these New Testament jigsaw pieces, or clues, with a degree of confidence as we legitimately consider whether they are relevant to the Rapture.

Concerning the coming of our Lord Jesus Christ and our being gathered to him, we ask you, brothers, not to become easily unsettled or alarmed by some prophecy, report or letter supposed to have come from us, saying that the day of the Lord has already come. Don't let anyone deceive you in any way, for that day will not come until the rebellion occurs and the man of lawlessness is revealed, the man doomed to destruction. He will oppose and will exalt himself over everything that is called God or is worshipped, so that he sets himself up in God's temple, proclaiming himself to be God.
Don't you remember that when I was with you I used to tell you these things? And now you know what is holding him back, so that he may be revealed at the proper time. For the secret power of lawlessness is already at work; but the one who now holds it back will continue to do so till he is taken out of the way. And then the lawless one will be revealed, whom the Lord Jesus will overthrow with the breath of his mouth and destroy by the splendour of his coming. The coming of the lawless one will be in accordance with the work of Satan displayed in all kinds of counterfeit miracles, signs and wonders, and in every sort of evil that deceives those who are perishing.

2 Thessalonians 2:1-10

This is one of the longest passages concerning the 'lawless one', 'the antichrist', 'the ruler to come' or 'the beast' found within the Bible. It refers to the end time preceding Jesus' coming, and it provides us with a clear chronology of events. Regarding the Rapture, we are first *'gathered to'* Christ, then the *'man of lawlessness'* is revealed along with the *'rebellion'*, who then causes the desolation of the Temple, which will all culminate in *'the day of the Lord'*.

The very fact that the readers of the letter had become alarmed is because they thought they had missed the Rapture, or being gathered to Christ. They were hearing false reports that *'the day of the Lord'* had already arrived, a term often used for a period of divine judgment as well as referring to the Glorious Appearing.

By having this scriptural record of the fears which the church in Thessalonica had, and Paul's response to it, we have been given another piece of evidence that Paul had been teaching a pre-Tribulation Rapture. It was because of this prior teaching that they were now alarmed, thinking they had missed the Rapture and that the *'day of the Lord'* had arrived already. If Paul had been teaching a mid- or post–Tribulation Rapture then his readers would not have been worried about the *'day of the Lord'* having already come.

In addition to this helpful sequence we can learn some further important truths from the clues within it. It is worth emphasising once again that Paul had previously taught them about eschatological matters.

Don't you remember that when I was with you I used to tell you these things?

2 Thessalonians 2:5

It can be argued that Paul had to leave Thessalonica before he was able to complete their eschatological education, and a reading of Paul's missionary troubles there in **Acts 17:1-13** might substantiate this. It is evident that this church had questions remaining which required Paul's teaching.

This proves the above point suggesting that Jesus, Paul, and maybe the other apostles too, knew much more about the Rapture, the Glorious Appearing, and the final judgment, than has been recorded in Scripture. Indeed, it also might cause us to thank God that Paul *was* moved on from Thessalonica prematurely so that Christians today can at least gain a basic understanding of such things from these written responses to questions.

To return to the above passage concerning the 'lawless one', there are further important truths which ought to be outlined. The next one is that there is one who is *'holding back'* the antichrist, preventing him from coming to power.

And now you know what is holding him back, so that he may be revealed at the proper time. For the secret power of lawlessness is already at work; but the one who now holds it back will continue to do so till he is taken out of the way.

2 Thessalonians 2:6-7

In a way, it is a shame that Paul's readers already knew to whom he was referring in this section, as it now leaves us to speculate. While some have suggested the 'restrainer' here is an angel, others have suggested the Church, and still others that the restrainer is the Holy Spirit or Jesus Christ. We cannot know for sure, but we may nevertheless draw attention to the detail.

For a start, we know that this was written after Christ's ascension, and after the Holy Spirit's powerful arriving at that Pentecost, so the restrainer is more likely to be the Holy Spirit than Jesus Christ. On the other hand, we can read here that the restrainer of the *'lawless one'* is referred to as a *'what'*, while the restrainer of the *'power of lawlessness'* is referred to as *'he'*.

64

There appears, then, to be two restraining influences, one described as 'what' the other described as 'he', but working together in restraining the rise of the 'man of lawlessness' and his power. It may therefore be possible that these verses are referring to both the Church *and* to the Holy Spirit. Due to lack of information or understanding we simply cannot identify these 'restrainers' for certain, but what we *are* certain of is that clearly Paul is teaching that before the antichrist can come onto the scene, something, *and* someone, needs to be taken out of the way.

Bearing in mind the whole context of the passage, one can understand the suggestion that this is a reference to the Rapture of the Church prior to the rise of the lawless one, and to a simultaneous withdrawal of the Church's 'Counsellor', our gift from the heavenly Father *(John 15:26)*. So, during the final seven years allotted to Israel the Holy Spirit's work is implemented as in Old Testament times. Naturally he would still be ministering within every new believer, just as he was prior to his powerful arrival on that Pentecost, but just as the Church age began so spectacularly, so it may well end with a similarly dramatic phenomenon.

This is not a perfect understanding of the text, but it is a distinct possibility as the combined removal of the restraining 'what' and 'who' is identified as the Rapture of the Church and the Holy Spirit.

Another feature to note from this helpful text is that the antichrist will be revealed 'at the proper time' (*2 Thessalonians 2:5*). This comes as a reminder that there is a definite order to end-time events, which will be brought to a close by the Glorious Appearing of Jesus Christ to defeat his enemies (*2 Thessalonians 2:8*).

It is very interesting, and relevant to this rationale, that the above passage found in Paul's second letter to the Thessalonians, based around an anxiety that the Rapture had already occurred, comes after his first letter to them in which we have one of our key Rapture texts (*1 Thessalonians 4:13-18*).

In other words, Paul writes to this church words of comfort based on a belief in the Rapture, and then has to write to them again because they had heard reports that the Rapture had already occurred. This merely adds to what is already a very credible Rapture concept.

Now, brothers, about times and dates we do not need to write to you, for you know very well that the day of the Lord will come like a thief in the night. While people are saying, 'Peace and safety', destruction will come on them suddenly, as labour pains on a pregnant woman, and they will not escape.
But you, brothers, are not in darkness so that this day should surprise you like a thief. You are all sons of the light and sons of the day. We do not belong to the night or to the darkness. So then, let us not be like others, who are asleep, but let us be alert and self-controlled. For those who sleep, sleep at night, and those who get drunk, get drunk at night. But since we belong to the day, let us be self-controlled, putting on faith and love as a breastplate, and the hope of salvation as a helmet. For God did not appoint us to suffer wrath but to receive salvation through our Lord Jesus Christ. He died for us so that, whether we are awake or asleep, we may live together with him. Therefore encourage one another and build each other up, just as in fact you are doing.

1 Thessalonians 5:1-11

This passage is found immediately after one of our key texts (*1 Thessalonians 4:13-18*), but has been left until now for consideration as it introduces the theme of God's wrath and whether Christians will escape it.

We notice that within the first two verses of this passage Paul is referring to something about which the readers have already been taught, '*we do not need to write ... for you know very well*'. This provides yet more evidence that his eschatological knowledge and teaching was more extensive than has been recorded.

We also notice in verse three that regarding the end-time it is '*while people are saying "Peace and safety"*' that destruction will come upon them, using the description of '*labour pains*' as Jesus did when describing the time of great distress (**Matthew 24:8**). The 'peace and safety' may well be a reference to the covenant confirmed with many, including Israel, which suddenly gets violated half-way through the time of Tribulation, as the '*man of lawlessness*' sets himself up in God's Temple (**2 Thessalonians 2:4**). This would also tie the following end-time Scripture together.

So when you see standing in the holy place 'the abomination that causes desolation', spoken of through the prophet Daniel – let the reader understand – then let those who are in Judea flee to the mountains.

Matthew 24:15, 16

He will confirm a covenant with many for one 'seven.' In the middle of the 'seven' he will put an end to sacrifice and offering. And on a wing of the temple he will set up an abomination that causes desolation, until the end that is decreed is poured out on him.

Daniel 9:27

The relevance of this to the Rapture comes directly after Paul mentions this time of 'destruction', because the very next paragraph starts with the words: '*But you...*' (**1 Thessalonians 5:4**). In other words a contrast is being made, and the readers are clearly being told that those caught in the time of 'destruction' do *not* include them, and the reason for their escape is based on what we read in verse nine.

For God did not appoint us to suffer wrath but to receive salvation through our Lord Jesus Christ.

1 Thessalonians 5:9

By acknowledging that there is a complete picture of end-time events, that an eschatological understanding had been previously taught by Paul, probably also by Jesus and possibly by others too, we can better understand the context in which Paul is writing. The readers understood that there will be a time in the future when 'peace and safety' seem to be guaranteed. They understand that it is during this time that destruction will come upon them as the lawless one breaks the covenant. This falls within the period of God's wrath, within seven years of Tribulation, but Paul is reminding his readers that they are exempt from that time.

Bearing in mind that **1 Thessalonians 5:1-11** comes directly after one of the key Scripture passages for the Rapture concept, we should interpret **1 Thessalonians 5:9** as teaching that Christians will escape the Tribulation, or God's appointed time of wrath. Therefore the whole section from **1 Thessalonians 4:13–5:11** is based on, and affirming, the hope of a pre-Tribulation Rapture. Any student of eschatology should read this whole passage with such a perspective, which will help many pieces of the Rapture puzzle to fall into place.

Without going into as much detail, this conclusion may also be reached by considering Paul's words at the beginning of this same letter, **1 Thessalonians 1:9-10:** *'You turned to God from idols to serve the living and true God, and to wait for his Son from Heaven, whom he raised from the dead – Jesus, who rescues us from the coming wrath.'*

Our previous studies mean that it is difficult to reason that *'the coming wrath'* could possibly be anything but the time of great Tribulation (**Revelation 7:14, Matthew 24:21**), when the judgments and catastrophes poured out upon the earth are repeatedly described as being a part of God's wrath (for example *Revelation 11:18, 14:10, 15:1, 15:7, 16:1, 16:19, 19:15*).

Then I heard a loud voice from the temple saying to the seven angels, 'Go, pour out the seven bowls of God's wrath on the earth.'
Revelation 16:1

The purpose of the wrath is best described in yet another possible piece of evidence toward a pre-Tribulation Rapture. Earlier in the same revelation, a message is given to the angel of the church in Philadelphia.

Since you have kept my command to endure patiently, I will also keep you from the hour of trial that is going to come upon the whole world to test those who live on the earth.
Revelation 3:10

This message from God provides a promise that those who belong to this church will be kept from God's coming wrath, here called the '*hour of trial*'. Here we can clearly see that the purpose of God's coming wrath is '*to test those who live on the earth*'.

It is a general wrath upon an unbelieving world, not to be confused with his individual wrath which is used to punish evil and ensure a just personal judgment. This wrath is large-scale, designed to make humankind aware that they are on the brink of his eternal judgment, reminding us that we have a choice of whether to accept or reject him.

Happily, the Tribulation accounts hint that such wrath will actually help vast numbers of people to turn to God, and to give him the glory (for example *Revelation 11:13*). A separate study of the book of Revelation, or on the seven years of Tribulation in particular, would soon discover that the horror which is the reality of facing God's wrath on earth is by no means intended to be a sadistic punishment of non-believers, instead it is an incredibly powerful reminder of God's omnipotence and sovereignty. This wrath acts as a reminder of his love as he provides a last chance for the world to recognise him.

The necessary fulfilment of the end-time prophecy requiring the gospel to be taken to all nations (**Mark 13:10**) will be finally fulfilled during this period, offering his gift of salvation to the whole world through faith alone in Jesus Christ.

Then I saw another angel flying in mid-air, and he had the eternal gospel to proclaim to those who live on the earth – to every nation, tribe, language and people. He said in a loud voice, 'Fear God and give him glory, because the hour of his judgment has come. Worship him who made the heavens, the earth, the sea and the springs of water.'

Revelation 14:6-7

The wrath of God, therefore, is double-edged. It is a general judgment on a non-believing world and a time of horrific catastrophes within a period of just seven years. It is also a demonstration of God's desire for people to turn to him who foresees our eternal future, and a time of blessing even as the gospel is taken to every nation. The evidence from the written responses about this time, however, indicate that the Church (everyone who has placed their trust in Jesus Christ to reconcile them to God), has been removed, taken, *'caught up'* to Heaven, and will indeed escape the coming wrath of God.

What Jesus said about wrath

This concept of escaping the coming wrath of God brings us back to considering one more thing Jesus said concerning a pre-Tribulation Rapture.

Just as it was in the days of Noah, so also will it be in the days of the Son of Man. People were eating, drinking, marrying and being given in marriage up to the day Noah entered the ark. Then the flood came and destroyed them all.

It was the same in the days of Lot. People were eating and drinking, buying and selling, planting and building. But the day Lot left Sodom, fire and sulfur rained down from heaven and destroyed them all.

It will be just like this on the day the Son of Man is revealed. On that day no one who is on the roof of his house, with his goods inside, should go down to get them. Likewise, no one in the field should go back for anything. Remember Lot's wife! Whoever tries to keep his life will lose it, and whoever loses his life will preserve it. I tell you, on that night two people will be in one bed; one will be taken and the other left. Two women will be grinding grain together; one will be taken and the other left.

Luke 17:26-35

While the start of this passage describes the world scene before and after the Rapture, the remainder depicts two separate events: *'on that day'* refers to the Glorious Appearing of Christ (**Luke 17:30-33**), and *'on that night'* refers to the Rapture when the Church is taken (**Luke 17:34-35**). It could be that no distinction is intended here, while others may question why Jesus used such an obvious contrast. Depending on one's outlook, it may be of no little consequence that in Jewish chronology *'night'* comes before *'day'*.

As for the end-time world scene, nothing unusual will be happening, as people will be eating and drinking, marrying, planting, building, selling, and investing in the future as if one day is the same as the next and will be forever more, until sudden disaster strikes. In the first scenario it is compared to the catastrophe of the great flood (**Genesis 6:5–9:1**). The second comparison is with the fire which came upon Sodom (**Genesis**

71

18:20–9:29). Both of these were clearly acts of divine judgment against wickedness, disbelief, and those lacking fear of God. In other words, they were acts of God's wrath.

The particularly interesting thing to note is that the righteous in each scenario are spared from God's wrath. Indeed, they have been spared in much the same way as the pre-Tribulation Rapture concept claims that righteous believers will be spared the coming wrath of God. Noah and his family were spared, as Lot was spared from Sodom's judgment. As we consider that it was Jesus Christ, knowing the future, who provided us with these words we can only assume that these examples were intentionally chosen to illustrate that believers in Jesus Christ will likewise escape the Tribulation.

More of what Paul wrote

Listen, I tell you a mystery: We will not all sleep, but we will all be changed – in a flash, in the twinkling of an eye, at the last trumpet. For the trumpet will sound, the dead will be raised imperishable, and we will be changed. For the perishable must clothe itself with the imperishable, and the mortal with immortality.

1 Corinthians 15:51-53

Our final text within this New Testament rationale based on the words of Jesus and the writings of Paul, returns to one of our key texts found in Paul's first letter to the Corinthians. Already we have examined this text and noted how, even on its own, it is a powerful piece of evidence for the Rapture. At the sound of the trumpet something will happen to the dead, and to the living, in that we shall be made immortal. We will not **all** sleep, that is, we will not all die, but we **will** all be changed. In other words, as the dead are raised imperishable, so those who are still alive will receive immortal bodies.

72

As far as the timing is concerned, and to stay within this letter from Paul to the Corinthians, we merely need to read the preceding paragraphs, starting at **1 Corinthians 15:1**.

Now, brothers, I want to remind you of the gospel I preached to you, which you received and on which you have taken your stand.

Paul then continues to outline the gospel, but seems intent throughout the whole chapter on proving the necessity of believing in the resurrection, of believers and indeed of Christ. Faith in the resurrection, for Paul, is an intrinsic part of the gospel he is preaching. This might be a further indication that to the Corinthians, too, Paul had previously provided eschatological teaching, including that on the Rapture.

With regard to the resurrection, then, Paul continues:

But Christ has indeed been raised from the dead, the firstfruits of those who have fallen asleep. For since death came through a man, the resurrection of the dead comes also through a man. For as in Adam all die, so in Christ all will be made alive.
But each in his own turn: Christ, the firstfruits; then, when he comes, those who belong to him. Then the end will come, when he hands over the Kingdom to God the Father after he has destroyed all dominion, authority and power. For he must reign until he has put all his enemies under his feet. The last enemy to be destroyed is death.

1 Corinthians 15:20-26

By analysing the order of resurrection we discover the chronology of future events, and all this within just a few sentences of Paul revealing the '*mystery*' of the Rapture.

First we have the resurrection of Christ, '*then, when he comes, those who belong to him*', in other words, Christians will be next, and then 'the end will come', which is *after he has destroyed all dominion, authority, and power*, and after he has reigned and *put all his enemies under his feet*.

From this sequence of events Paul is saying that the next event is for Christians to be resurrected, and then for various other things to happen. Christ will deal with his enemies, reign a while, destroy other dominions and powers, including death itself, and then hand the Kingdom over to God the Father. The 'next event' within this sequence is Christ resurrecting those who belong to him. This sounds extraordinarily similar to a pre-Tribulation Rapture, along with a time of Tribulation and judgment, followed by a Millennial Kingdom, followed by eternity in Heaven. All these pieces fit precisely with a futurist interpretation of the book of Revelation.

This chapter is concerned with the actual timing of the Rapture. Paul is teaching a pre-Tribulation viewpoint which has a fairly solid argument from *1 Corinthians 15* alone. So let us piece it together.

1 Corinthians 15:20-26 is our evidence that the next event within the gospel story is the resurrection of Christians, before any other end-time events.

1 Corinthians 15:51-53 is our evidence that when the dead in Christ are *changed* then those who are still alive will be *changed* too, from perishable to imperishable, from mortal to immortal, and '*in the twinkling of an eye*'.

Scripture does not provide any evidence for Christians being changed into immortal bodies and yet being kept on earth throughout the Tribulation period. Neither does Scripture advocate a belief that there will be a future event when the dead will be changed and 'taken up' to Heaven, but not those who are still alive.

By putting these two short passages together, we can see that Paul was preaching a gospel which included the resurrection of dead Christians with new imperishable bodies as being 'the next event'. Living Christians will have their bodies transformed *'in a flash'* at this same event, followed by various other end-time scenarios. Not only do these words from Paul confirm the pre-Tribulation Rapture idea, but they make any contrasting theory very difficult to sustain.

There are many more New Testament pieces of the 'puzzle' which also confirm the concept. These will be listed further in this study. Within this section, however, a rationale has been offered which is based upon the words and writings of Jesus Christ and the apostle Paul as a starting point which includes an analysis of the key texts. Both of them appear to have taught about the Rapture to their followers and churches, and it is of immense benefit to us that some of this teaching has been recorded and reflected in Scripture.

We can summarise this part of the study by simply saying that the New Testament apostle Paul evidently taught about eschatological matters when he visited the Early Church. The Bible has recorded some of both Paul's and Jesus' responses to questions regarding the end-times, and this has enabled us to piece together their teaching. In doing so we have uncovered plenty of evidence to substantiate the proposal that both Paul and Jesus taught about the Rapture, or the gathering of the Church to Christ. Furthermore, this biblical rationale, based purely on Jesus' words and Paul's letters to the Thessalonians and Corinthians, asserts that the pre-Tribulation viewpoint is the most satisfactory.

An Old Testament rationale

This rationale is based upon a prophetic analysis of the appointed feasts of Israel which are listed in **Leviticus 23**. It is an extremely important chapter of the Torah within Judaism. Due to the size of the passage we shall be examining it in brief, taking one festival at a time, but the reader may want to proceed by first reading the whole of the passage in order to gain an understanding of its context, including the importance of these seven feasts to every Jew.

I am indebted to the Jewish End-time Ministries Director Dr Steve Cook for having first introduced me to the prophetic nature of this chapter, and also to websites such as www.torah.org and www.askmoses.org which have helped me confirm how this important piece of Scripture is practised within Judaism.

The Bible is a Jewish book, written predominantly by Jewish authors, mainly to Jewish readers, with its focus on the Jewish Messiah, Jesus Christ. The Jews were a special race, a chosen people, and there is good reason to believe they will continue to be so. Some of God's covenants with the Jewish people and their ancestors were not conditional, which means such covenants could not be broken by the disbelief or disobedience of Israel. However, it has been God's pleasure to make his salvation, indwelling and blessings available to Gentiles too, through the sacrificial death and resurrection of Jesus Christ.

Because of this, anyone may come to God through faith in what Jesus has done, and trusting in the free gift of salvation which the New Testament teaches. However, biblical eschatology reveals that God has not finished with the Jewish race. There are also matters which seem to be particularly intended for Jews in the Old Testament which have profound importance and relevance to all of God's people, including non-Jews, today. The establishment of the appointed Jewish feasts is an example of this.

Although a proper study of these appointed feasts thoroughly deserves a book of its own, this chapter will describe how it can be argued that these lasting ordinances (some of which predate the Old Covenant of the Decalogue) not only have the purpose of being memorials to what God has done, but are also prophetic in nature and tell of what God will do.

Introducing the seven appointed feasts of Leviticus 23

Just as the number seven often indicates completeness within Scripture, so these seven appointed feasts may prophesy the complete gospel of Christ, from his first coming as the suffering Messiah to his Glorious Appearing as King of kings. Jesus Christ is their fulfilment, in what he has already done, and in what he will do. By outlining these feasts and their prophetic relevance we may catch a glimpse of the place of the Rapture within God's prophetic timescale.

These appointed feasts, then, have a twofold purpose. To Israel, the seven feasts provided reminders of how merciful and gracious Jehovah had been to them as a nation. They served not only as a means by which their identity could be maintained, even when dispersed, but they also helped them in their personal and collective spiritual relationship with God. Every time these feasts were practised the Jews recalled what he had done for them.

To the Church, the same seven feasts provide us with a magnificent picture of Christ, and his fulfilment of God's prophetic timetable, some of which has occurred, and some which has yet to pass. Ultimately these feasts provide the Christian with a heightened sense of trust in a God who is in control of all things.

It is helpful constantly to bear in mind that it was God himself who instituted these feasts. Their observance was to continue forever. His words regarding them are a lasting ordinance, and we can legitimately assume that God had a reason for demanding their implementation which would be in keeping with his story as a part of his eternal plan.

It is my hope that through the brief descriptions of these feasts readers will concur that there are too many 'coincidences' to call them anything but a demonstration of God's perfect plan and foreknowledge. A pre-Tribulation Rapture concept will be proposed through this remarkable passage and its gospel comparisons.

The timing of the appointed feasts

These are the LORD's appointed feasts, the sacred assemblies you are to proclaim at their appointed times

Leviticus 23:4

The first three appointed feasts are those of the Passover, the Feast of Unleavened Bread and the Feast of Firstfruits. These are very closely related, and accordingly they are observed in the first month of the Jewish calendar, Nisan.

The last three feasts are those of the Day of Trumpets, the Day of Atonement and the Feast of Tabernacles. These are also closely related, and accordingly they are observed in the seventh month of the Jewish calendar, Tishri.

Between these two groups is the fourth feast called the Feast of Pentecost. The first four feasts also had the purpose of prophesying the gospel and *have been* amazingly fulfilled by Christ in the past. The last three feasts also have the purpose of prophesying the gospel, and *will be* amazingly fulfilled by Christ in the future.

To make the connection between the appointed feasts, their prophetic nature and gospel fulfilment, we need to understand that every detail of God's ordinances has meaning. **Leviticus 23** is full of types and shadows of what was to come. The New Testament confirms this regularly, as if to indicate that it is only once every God-ordained requirement of the Old Testament is understood within the context of Jesus Christ that its full meaning can be revealed.

At this point it would be extremely helpful to read through **Colossians 2:1-23**. With the above in mind we can understand the message that Paul, a devout Jew, was trying to get across. His whole belief system made sense and was given meaning once he came to Christ. Though the whole chapter is worth studying, perhaps verse 17 is the best summary of Paul's understanding of the Old Testament regulations.

These are a shadow of the things that were to come; the reality, however, is found in Christ.
Colossians 2:17

Similarly, we find that the tabernacle which Moses built was so detailed for a good reason, and again the law merely foreshadowed what was to come.

They serve at a sanctuary that is a copy and shadow of what is in Heaven. This is why Moses was warned when he was about to build the tabernacle: 'See to it that you make everything according to the pattern shown you on the mountain.'
Hebrews 8:5

The law is only a shadow of the good things that are coming – not the realities themselves.

Hebrews 10:1

In the same way, these seven appointed feasts foreshadowed what was to come. They had prophetic qualities. Just as God's provision and the 'religious calendar' of Israel is the subject of **Leviticus 23**, so it foreshadows, or predicts God's eternal provision through Christ and his 'prophetic calendar' and perfect timing.

The chapter and its feasts contain many references to keeping Sabbath days, or sacred assemblies, and the passage starts with a reminder of the Sabbath's importance before we get to the first of the seven appointed feasts.

The Feast of Passover

These are the LORD's appointed feasts, the sacred assemblies you are to proclaim at their appointed times: The LORD's Passover begins at twilight on the fourteenth day of the first month.

Leviticus 23:4-5

Not much is stated here concerning this first feast. It refers to a well known and understood act of remembrance concerning the redemption of the Israelites from their slavery in Egypt. In a final act of persuasion from God to the Egyptian Pharaoh, as well as being a sign to the Jews of God's faithfulness, power and provision, the angel of the Lord would literally 'pass over' the homes of the Israelites as it killed the firstborn in every remaining household, including the palace. The Israelites escaped because they had followed God's instruction through Moses to kill a lamb and smear its blood on the doorposts and lintels of their homes. In effect, *the blood of the lamb* is what saved them from their bondage as Pharaoh then agreed to let the Israelites leave his land.

This act was to be remembered as a lasting ordinance, and may not have been listed in detail here as it was described more fully in Exodus 12. We find there that on the 10th day of the first month (Nisan), each Jewish family would choose a lamb, without spot or blemish, and observe it for four days (**Exodus 12**) before it was killed and eaten. Every year this would be an act which would remind the Israelites of the salvation God provided as he rescued his people from slavery.

However, it was also an annual prophetic reminder that God would provide the ultimate salvation from the slavery of sin, through the sacrifice of his own Lamb without blemish, Jesus Christ. Even before Jesus began his ministry this prophecy was understood by those who were anticipating his salvation.

The next day John saw Jesus coming toward him and said, 'Look, the Lamb of God, who takes away the sin of the world!'
John 1:29

John the Baptist evidently understood the prophetic meaning behind the Passover feast, which as a Jew he would have also observed in obedience to **Leviticus 23**. Again, the apostle Paul, a devout Jew who observed the Jewish law, understood the prophetic fulfillment of the Passover feast that was achieved through Jesus' sacrifice.

For Christ, our Passover lamb, has been sacrificed. Therefore let us keep the Festival, not with the old yeast, the yeast of malice and wickedness, but with bread without yeast, the bread of sincerity and truth.
1 Corinthians 5:6-8

It is also interesting to note that Paul seems to be advocating that Jews should continue to '*keep the Festival*', as it was '*a lasting ordinance*' (**Exodus 12:24**). Yet there is no doubt that both Paul and John saw Jesus as being the fulfillment of that feast, and as being the prophetic purpose behind it.

Elsewhere in the New Testament this Old Testament prophecy is affirmed as Christ is repeatedly called *'the Lamb that was slain'* (for example **Revelation 5:12; 13:2**), or simply *'the Lamb'*. Just like the original lambs he was killed at Passover (**John 19:14**), the timing was perfect, and in the light of this feast's prophetic nature it should also come as no surprise that the book of Revelation refers to Jesus Christ as *'the Lamb'* no fewer than 27 times.

The festival of the Passover clearly depicts the sacrificial death of Christ who became the ultimate Passover Lamb, the Lamb of God, without 'blemish', through whose blood we have been rescued from sin and identified as belonging to God.

It is plain to see that these are not mere similarities, but that the words recorded in **Leviticus 23** contained both lasting ordinances for the Jews, and also words of prophecy from God about how his gospel would be fulfilled in the future.

The Passover feast foreshadowed a future event, which was accurately fulfilled by Jesus Christ. This encourages us to know that God is in control. He must have had the future in mind when declaring the necessity of observing the Passover. He could have simply 'passed over' the Israelites without the slaughter of lambs but his ordinances had a distinct prophetic teaching purpose. If this is true of the feast of Passover, then it is reasonable for us to suspect it may also be true of the other six appointed feasts of **Leviticus 23**.

The Feast of Unleavened Bread

On the fifteenth day of that month the LORD's Feast of Unleavened Bread begins; for seven days you must eat bread made without yeast. *On the first day hold a sacred assembly and do no regular work. For seven days present an offering made to the LORD by fire. And on the seventh day hold a sacred assembly and do no regular work.*

Leviticus 23:6-8

The Feast of Unleavened Bread took place immediately after, and sometimes was celebrated hand-in-hand with, Passover. While Passover was to be observed every year on 14th Nisan, this annual feast begins on the next day, 15th Nisan, and continues for seven days until the 21st day of that first month. During this feast, no leaven or yeast was to be eaten, and bread made without yeast must be eaten. This feast was an annual remembrance of what God prescribed to the Israelites at the original Passover, and reminds the Jews of the speed with which they were then able to leave their captors.

This is a day you are to commemorate; for the generations to come you shall celebrate it as a festival to the LORD – a lasting ordinance. For seven days you are to eat bread made without yeast. On the first day remove the yeast from your houses, for whoever eats anything with yeast in it from the first day through the seventh must be cut off from Israel. On the first day hold a sacred assembly, and another one on the seventh day. Do no work at all on these days, except to prepare food for everyone to eat – that is all you may do.

Exodus 12:14-16

Just as the Passover foreshadowed a reality that was revealed in Christ, so the Feast of Unleavened Bread can only be prophetically understood by considering it within the context of the New Testament following Christ's sacrifice. At this point read through **1 Corinthians 5.** This passage provides a context for the key verses with regard to the meaning of this feast, describing yeast as something bad, and sinful, which can spread.

Your boasting is not good. Don't you know that a little yeast works through the whole batch of dough? Get rid of the old yeast that you may be a new batch without yeast – as you really are. For Christ, our Passover lamb, has been sacrificed. Therefore let us keep the Festival, not with the old yeast, the yeast of malice and wickedness, but with bread without yeast, the bread of sincerity and truth.

1 Corinthians 5:6-8

Paul uses the same illustration of yeast being equated to sin in **Galatians 5:9,** but in **Matthew 13:33** Jesus used yeast to describe the expansion of the Kingdom of heaven, so care must be taken not to assume yeast is always symbolic of something bad. However, further on in **Matthew 16:6-12** Jesus again refers to yeast, this time symbolising false teaching.

'But be on your guard against the yeast of the Pharisees and Sadducees.' Then they understood that he was not telling them to guard against the yeast used in bread, but against the teaching of the Pharisees and Sadducees.

In the main, then, yeast in the New Testament is used to refer to something sinful or unholy, and certainly Paul's first letter to the Corinthians in which he describes Christ as being the Passover Lamb, simultaneously interprets yeast as being representative of sinfulness.

What was God telling his chosen people through this feast? If it is prophetic, what does the Feast of Unleavened Bread foreshadow? The New Testament rarely mentions the Feast, except either as an extension of the Passover Feast or twice within historical accounts which help achieve some sort of timeframe or social climate (**Acts 12:3; 20:6**). Other than this, the most obvious reference to the feast is the one mentioned by Paul in **1 Corinthians 5**, where leaven, or yeast, is depicted as being symbolic of sin.

84

The *Exodus 12* passage gives the impression that the Feast of Unleavened Bread was not only an act of preparation and remembrance for God's leading of the Israelites out of Egypt in the past, but was also symbolic of the need to prepare ourselves for God's leading in the future.

Just as any trace of yeast had to be cleared out of the home within Judaism, so Christ calls us to clear out any trace of sin in our hearts and lives. This feast illustrates that our life should be free from all sin and malice. Those who have placed their trust in the blood of the Lamb are indeed considered holy, acceptable to God and 'yeast free', even while we are still in the process of striving for such holiness.

Without the Passover Feast, the Feast of Unleavened Bread would not take place. Without the blood of the Lamb of God, we would be stuck in Egypt, and in slavery. Without trust in Jesus Christ' death, our sins would not be forgiven, and holiness would be forever unattainable.

But this was only a shadow of the reality, which is that Christ *is* our Passover. He *is* the Lamb whose blood saves us, and because of this we are now called to be a holy people, striving toward holiness, clearing out any trace of sin, but knowing we are already forgiven.

Therefore, if the Passover Feast was prophetic of Christ being our Passover Lamb, the Feast of Unleavened Bread is prophetic of our need to strive for holiness. Just as there is no break in time between the Feasts of Passover and Unleavened Bread, so there should be no break in time between our salvation and our striving for holiness. At the moment of our salvation the Holy Spirit takes over in our heart and we need to let him have a good clear out.

Yet again we see that the Law which can sometimes seem so baffling and over-meticulous is, in the seven prophetic feasts of Israel, a shadow of the reality which is Jesus Christ.

The Feast of the Passover prophesied the Lamb of God, Jesus Christ, who was sacrificed for us. The Feast of Unleavened Bread prophesied both the need and ability to strive for holiness, with immediate effect, through the help of the Holy Spirit.

The Feast of 'Firstfruit'

The LORD said to Moses, 'Speak to the Israelites and say to them: "When you enter the land I am going to give you and you reap its harvest, bring to the priest a sheaf of the first grain you harvest. He is to wave the sheaf before the LORD so it will be accepted on your behalf; the priest is to wave it on the day after the Sabbath. On the day you wave the sheaf, you must sacrifice as a burnt offering to the LORD a lamb a year old without defect, together with its grain offering of two-tenths of an ephah of fine flour mixed with oil – an offering made to the LORD by fire, a pleasing aroma – and its drink offering of a quarter of a hin of wine. You must not eat any bread, or roasted or new grain, until the very day you bring this offering to your God. This is to be a lasting ordinance for the generations to come, wherever you live."'

Leviticus 23:9-14

If each of these holy times has a unique purpose, they are appointed for a reason, and if the Passover foreshadowed the death of Christ, then the Feast of Firstfruits, sometimes called the Feast of the First Grain, the Beginning of Harvest, or the Wave Sheaf offering, was similarly prophesying his resurrection.

It would occur immediately after the first weekly Sabbath during the Feast of Unleavened Bread, and would mark the beginning of the spring harvest. We know that it is the weekly Sabbath that is intended as the guide, because the annual Sabbaths at the beginning and end of the Feast of Unleavened Bread could fall on

86

any day of the week, and yet Pentecost (50 days after this Feast) must fall on the beginning of the week – a Sunday (*Leviticus 23:15-16*).

Many years later, the first weekly Sabbath after Jesus was killed naturally preceded the first day of the week – Sunday. We know that it was early on this day that he was resurrected (*Luke 24:1-6*). Therefore, just as the Bible tells us that Jesus died at Passover, fulfilling that Feast's prophecy, so we know that he came back to life again on the Feast of First Grain or Firstfruits. This is no coincidence. Christ died at an 'appointed time', and Christ arose at an 'appointed time'. God's eternal plan was being worked out.

Just as the Old Testament priest would have brought this first sheaf of the harvest and waved it before the Lord as an initial offering of what was to follow, so Jesus was the first offering of those who would be resurrected, making us acceptable to God.

This helps us to understand Jesus' words to Mary early that resurrection morning:

Jesus said, 'Do not hold on to me, for I have not yet returned to the Father.'

John 20:17

Jesus said this because he was about to fulfill the ancient requirements of the Beginning of Harvest, the First Grain offering. Because of his fulfilment of all these first three appointed feasts, all the subsequent 'harvest' of his resurrected believers will likewise be acceptable to God.

But Christ has indeed been raised from the dead, the firstfruits of those who have fallen asleep.

1 Corinthians 15:20

This rationale contends that Paul did not call Jesus the 'firstfruits' by accident, nor by coincidence, but because of the very knowledge that the appointed feast under that name was fulfilled by Jesus.

Jesus said, 'I am the resurrection and the life. He who believes in me will live, even though he dies; and whoever lives and believes in me will never die.'

John 11:25-26

The Feast of Pentecost

From the day after the Sabbath, the day you brought the sheaf of the wave offering, count off seven full weeks. Count off fifty days up to the day after the seventh Sabbath, and then present an offering of new grain to the LORD. From wherever you live, bring two loaves made of two-tenths of an ephah of fine flour, baked with yeast, as a wave offering of firstfruits to the LORD. Present with this bread seven male lambs, each a year old and without defect, one young bull and two rams. They will be a burnt offering to the LORD, together with their grain offerings and drink offerings – an offering made by fire, an aroma pleasing to the LORD. Then sacrifice one male goat for a sin offering and two lambs, each a year old, for a fellowship offering. The priest is to wave the two lambs before the LORD as a wave offering, together with the bread of the firstfruits. They are a sacred offering to the LORD for the priest. On that same day you are to proclaim a sacred assembly and do no regular work. This is to be a lasting ordinance for the generations to come, wherever you live.

Leviticus 23:15-22

Having examined the first three feasts, we now come to the fourth – the Feast of Pentecost. Given the astounding way in which God foreknew and foretold his plan of salvation through the first three appointed Feasts, we may assume that the Feast of Pentecost is also prophetic in nature.

This fourth feast is called by a variety of names – Pentecost (Greek for 50); Feast of Weeks; Feast of Harvest; or Shavuot (Hebrew for Feast of Weeks). Our passage tells us that it was ordained to be celebrated exactly 50 days after the Feast of Firstfruits.

From the day after the Sabbath, the day you brought the sheaf of the wave offering, count off seven full weeks. Count off fifty days up to the day after the seventh Sabbath, and then present an offering of new grain to the LORD.

Leviticus 23:15, 16

It was observed not only in thanksgiving for the spring harvest, but in remembrance of the giving of the Law. Following the Hebrews' Exodus from Egypt and their miraculous escape through the Red Sea, the Israelites travelled on until they arrived at Mount Sinai, at which point God instructed Moses to have the people purify themselves.

At the end of their 47-day journey from Egypt, they purified themselves for three days, resulting in a total of 50 days, hence the word Pentecost. We can be absolutely certain of these time-frames by examining **Exodus 19-20**. Exactly 50 days after the first weekly Sabbath after the original Passover, Moses received the Decalogue from God on Mount Sinai. Pentecost reminds us of this.

Here comes the astounding parallel – exactly 50 days after Christ rose from the dead in fulfilment of the Feast of First Grain, the disciples were gathered in Jerusalem, as were thousands of visitors, because it was time to celebrate the Jewish requirement of Pentecost, the Feast of Weeks. It is on that day that Christ's gift of the Holy Spirit came down upon them, and became the law written within their hearts.

When the day of Pentecost came, they were all together in one place. Suddenly a sound like the blowing of a violent wind came from heaven and filled the whole house where they were sitting. They saw what seemed to be tongues of fire that separated and came to rest on each of them. All of them were filled with the Holy Spirit and began to speak in other tongues as the Spirit enabled them.
Now there were staying in Jerusalem God-fearing Jews from every nation under heaven. When they heard this sound, a crowd came together in bewilderment, because each one heard them speaking in his own language.

Acts 2:1-6

In the Old Testament we read how God dealt with the Jewish people as a precise mirror image of what he would do through Jesus Christ. God's appointed feasts accurately continued to foreshadow what was to come within his plan of salvation. Once again we find that the Feast of Weeks is no exception. In addition to being a feast of thanksgiving and memorial, exactly 50 days after the Feast of First Grain, it was a prophecy. Exactly 50 days after Christ became the firstfruits of the resurrection, exactly 50 days after he fulfilled the prophetic meaning behind the Feast of First Grain, he went on to fulfil the Feast of Weeks by sending us the gift of the Holy Spirit.

Many more amazing parallels can be recognised. For now, however, we may highlight just one further parallel of confirmation that the original Pentecost and the day of the Holy Spirit's arrival have mirror-like qualities.

We are told that 3,000 Israelites perished for their sin on the day the Law came down at Mt Sinai.

90

Moses saw that the people were running wild and that Aaron had let them get out of control and so become a laughingstock to their enemies. So he stood at the entrance to the camp and said, 'Whoever is for the LORD, come to me.' And all the Levites rallied to him.
Then he said to them, 'This is what the LORD, the God of Israel, says: "Each man strap a sword to his side. Go back and forth through the camp from one end to the other, each killing his brother and friend and neighbour." The Levites did as Moses commanded, and that day about three thousand of the people died.

Exodus 32:25-28

With incredible similarity, on this same day of Pentecost in Israel's calendar, which many centuries later marked the arrival of the Holy Spirit upon the Church, the first Christians were empowered and Peter preached the forgiveness of sins boldly, resulting in 3,000 souls being saved – both Jew and Gentile.

'Therefore let all Israel be assured of this: God has made this Jesus, whom you crucified, both Lord and Christ.'
When the people heard this, they were cut to the heart and said to Peter and the other apostles, 'Brothers, what shall we do?'
Peter replied, 'Repent and be baptised, every one of you, in the name of Jesus Christ for the forgiveness of your sins. And you will receive the gift of the Holy Spirit. The promise is for you and your children and for all who are far off – for all whom the Lord our God will call.'
With many other words he warned them; and he pleaded with them, 'Save yourselves from this corrupt generation.' Those who accepted his message were baptised, and about three thousand were added to their number that day.

Acts 2:36-41

This precise reflection of the number 3,000 comes almost like a gentle reminder from the Author of this whole story, a confirmation that he is in complete control. A further indication that Pentecost, celebrating the receiving of the Law by Moses from Mt Sinai, was a foreshadow of a future event. It was a divine prophecy, finding fulfillment 50 days after Christ released us from death, as he sent his Holy Spirit to put the law into our hearts and minds, our seal of the new covenant.

The Feast Day of Trumpets

These are the LORD's appointed feasts, the sacred assemblies you are to proclaim at their appointed times

Leviticus 23:4

So far, then, we have considered the prophetic relevance and meaning of the first four appointed feasts: the Passover, the Feast of Unleavened Bread, the Feast of Firstfruits and the Feast of Pentecost.

We have identified the parallels with New Testament teaching. We have shown that the first four feasts also had the purpose of prophesying the gospel of Christ, and have been fulfilled by Christ through his sacrificial death, victory over sin, resurrection and gift of the Holy Spirit respectively.

It is, therefore, wise to expect that the final three feasts also have the purpose of prophesying the gospel, and will similarly be fulfilled by Christ in the future. The New Testament confirms this as if to indicate that it is only once every God-ordained requirement of the Old Testament is understood within the context of Jesus Christ that its full meaning can be revealed.

These are a shadow of the things that were to come; the reality, however, is found in Christ.

Colossians 2:17

92

By this reckoning, the fifth feast, then, must foreshadow the 'next event' in God's prophetic calendar. Let us, therefore, examine whether the Day of Trumpets may in some way foreshadow the Rapture of the Church.

The law is only a shadow of the good things that are coming – not the realities themselves.
Hebrews 10:1

Say to the Israelites: 'On the first day of the seventh month you are to have a day of rest, a sacred assembly commemorated with trumpet blasts. Do no regular work, but present an offering made to the LORD by fire.'
Leviticus 23:24-25

This fifth feast was to be celebrated on the first day of the seventh month, Tishri. Therefore between each of the feasts mentioned, the largest time period is found between that of Pentecost and the Feast Day of Trumpets. Similarly, nearly 2,000 years after the fulfilment of the Passover Feast, we are still waiting for the fulfilment of the next event.

On the first day of the seventh month hold a sacred assembly and do no regular work. It is a day for you to sound the trumpets.
Numbers 29:1

The term Day of Trumpets is, in Hebrew, *Yom Teruah*. The trumpets often consisted of ram's horns (for example **Joshua 6:4**), called, in Hebrew, the *shofar*. Any kosher animal's horns may be used, except those of a cow. At this feast the *shofar* would be sounded many times in various sequences, but what is important to this book is that the last call of the *shofar* during this feast is called the *Tekiah Gedolah*, which is Hebrew for the final 'big blast'. This blast is particularly long and loud.

93

The *shofar* itself has a unique sound, and sometimes the final blast comes after a sequence of 30 other smaller blasts, and sometimes as many as 100 blasts are heard on each day of this celebration. The event commemorates the creation of the world, and especially of Adam and his relationship to God. Therefore, although it falls in the seventh month of the civil calendar, its celebration of Creation marks it as the beginning of the religious New Year, *Rosh Hashanah*.

The purpose of the *shofar*-blowing is twofold, firstly to 'awaken' the listeners from their spiritual slumber, and secondly to call Israel to 10 days of repentance (in Hebrew *Teshuvah*), culminating in the next celebration, the Day of Atonement. Accordingly, the notes from the *shofar* can have either a joyful or wailing sound.

So the first day of the seventh month, the Feast Day of Trumpets, includes the blowing of many blasts of the *shofar* or 'trumpet'. It comes to a close with the blowing of the Tekiah Gedolah, which is the final, or last trumpet to sound. This ceremony lasts for 48 hours (first and second Tishrei, due to uncertainty over the appearance of the New Moon), but to meet scriptural requirements is considered to be one long day. Then there is a further seven-day period of repentance and spiritual introspection before the Day of Atonement, *Yom Kippur*, arrives on 10th Tishrei.

The parallels between this Day of Trumpets and its prophetic fulfilment within God's plan of salvation are just as amazing as the previous four feasts. Despite the fact that we are literally entering into unknown territory, in that these last three feasts are in the future, we can nonetheless clearly perceive how the next event within God's prophetic calendar, the Rapture, has been foreshadowed by this fifth feast.

Firstly, we have the most obvious parallel on which this Old Testament rationale for the Rapture concept is based – the reference to trumpets. Some people may think there are too many references to trumpets to be able to identify their meaning and relevance. Others think the connection between the Rapture and the use of trumpets is found in the scriptural use of trumpets when going into battle (for example **Numbers 10:8, 9**), or when Moses led the people out of the camp to meet with God (**Exodus 19:16-19**), or when Joshua used trumpets to gain access to the promised land (**Joshua 6:20**). All these examples are possibilities which may illustrate a link between trumpets and the Rapture. However, I believe the truth is much stronger and more profound than any of these suggestions. It relies on the simple belief that the Day of Trumpets is an appointed feast with equally significant prophetic qualities to the previous four feasts.

The Day of Trumpets is significant. The significance lies in the blowing of the last *shofar* of the feast, the Tekiah Gedolah, the long, loud, final blast. It would appear that this trumpet is the one that Paul was referring to when he wrote:

Listen, I tell you a mystery: we will not all sleep, but we will all be changed – in a flash, in the twinkling of an eye, at **the last trumpet**. *For the trumpet will sound, the dead will be raised imperishable, and we will be changed. For the perishable must clothe itself with the imperishable, and the mortal with immortality.*

1 Corinthians 15:51-53

God has a moment scheduled in the future when the last trumpet will sound, fulfilling the final long blast of the *shofar* at the Day of Trumpets.

Without this understanding of Paul's words, we could easily become confused as to what he meant when he specified the '*last* trumpet'. It is evident, for example, that at Christ's glorious appearing there shall be the sound of a trumpet (**Matthew 24:31**), and throughout the first half of the Tribulation we read of seven heavenly trumpets of wrath being blown (**Revelation 8:7-11:15**).

We also know that Paul could not have been referring to the *Shofar Hagadol* of **Isaiah 27:13** because then he would have simply called it, the '*great* trumpet' and avoided any confusion. Instead he deliberately chose to call it the *last* trumpet, despite the fact that there are clearly more trumpets to follow.

So his readers have a choice. When Paul spoke of the Rapture occurring at '*the last trumpet*' he was either mistaken, or talking about something other than a Rapture or he was using the word 'last' within a different context rather than 'for all time and for all occasions'.

This Old Testament rationale asserts that Paul's use of the phrase '*the last trumpet*' refers directly to the final blast of the *shofar* at this feast, and that this future event will be the fulfilment of the Day of Trumpets. This joyous celebration is prophesying the next event within God's 'story'. There is no doubt that after the event has occurred then those who study the parallels will be as amazed at the prophetic nature of the Feast as we have been by studying the previous four Feasts. However, there is more evidence from what we know of Scripture which helps confirm this in advance.

We need to consider the reason for the *shofar* blowing. Its very sound and purpose is intended to 'awaken' the listener from spiritual slumber, as well as being a call to repentance. Again we may refer to Paul's words to the Corinthians, as above, as well as to his words to the Thessalonians:

Brothers, we do not want you to be ignorant about **those who fall asleep**, *or to grieve like the rest of men, who have no hope. We believe that Jesus died and rose again and so we believe that God will bring with Jesus* **those who have fallen asleep in him**.

According to the Lord's own word, we tell you that we who are still alive, who are left till the coming of the Lord, will certainly not precede **those who have fallen asleep.** *For the Lord himself will come down from heaven, with a loud command, with the voice of the archangel and with* **the trumpet call of God,** *and the dead in Christ will rise first. After that, we who are still alive and are left will be caught up together with them in the clouds to meet the Lord in the air. And so we will be with the Lord forever. Therefore encourage each other with these words.*

1 Thessalonians 4:13-18

In both instances those who have died but had placed their faith in Christ are described as being 'asleep'. In both instances the trumpet call of God is what 'awakens' them to rise at the Rapture. The awakening call of the final *shofar* predicts and foreshadows the call of the last trumpet. The Day of Trumpets predicts and foreshadows the Rapture of the Church.

'Say to the Israelites: "On the first day of the seventh month you are to have a day of rest, a sacred assembly commemorated with trumpet blasts. Do no regular work, but present an offering made to the LORD by fire."'

Leviticus 23:24-25

On the first day of the seventh month hold a sacred assembly and do no regular work. It is a day for you to sound the trumpets.

Numbers 29:1

But this last call of the *shofar* is twofold, and it is also a prophecy regarding Israel's final week of years. Just as the blast of the *shofar* has an element of joy and awakening, so it has its wailing call to repent and seek God afresh. Once again the resemblance to what we know of eschatology would encourage us to consider that while the last trumpet calls Christ's Bride, the Church, to Heaven, so it calls Israel to repentance and spiritual renewal, giving the Jewish race a final chance, a 'week' of years to recognise Jesus as Messiah.

It may be pure coincidence that between the celebration of *Rosh Hashanah* and the Day of Atonement, our next appointed festival, there are precisely seven days. What is not coincidental is that just as the Rapture and Christ's glorious appearing can only be fully understood in relation to each other, so the Feast Day of Trumpets, or *Rosh Hashanah*, and the Day of Atonement can only be fully understood in relation to each other.

If, therefore, within Paul's first letter to the Corinthians, the resurrection and rapture passage of chapter 15 was written with this appointed Feast Day of Trumpets in mind, we might expect to find further supportive evidence to this effect. Such evidence comes as we recall that this Feast Day was instigated as a celebration in memorial of Creation, and in particular of Adam and his special relationship to God.

So it is written: 'The first man Adam became a living being'; the last Adam, a life-giving spirit. The spiritual did not come first, but the natural, and after that the spiritual. The first man was of the dust of the earth, the second man from Heaven. As was the earthly man, so are those who are of the earth; and as is the man from Heaven, so also are those who are of Heaven. And just as we have borne the likeness of the earthly man, so shall we bear the likeness of the man from Heaven.

1 Corinthians 15:45-49

This reference to Adam's creation comes immediately before our main Rapture text from **1 Corinthians 15:50-54**, in which we have that all-important reference to '*the last trumpet*' in verse 52. Surely this can be for no other reason than because the Feast Day of Trumpets is the common denominator. This is in perfect consistency with the rest of the chapter, and indeed the letter, in which we also find that Paul describes how the other appointed Feasts have been fulfilled.

Christ is our Passover:

For Christ, our Passover lamb, has been sacrificed.
1 Corinthians 5:7

Christ has defeated sin, enabling us to strive for the 'unleavened bread' of holiness:

Therefore let us keep the festival, not with the old yeast, the yeast of malice and wickedness, but with bread without yeast, the bread of sincerity and truth.
1 Corinthians 5:8

Christ fulfilled the Feast of First Grain:

But Christ has indeed been raised from the dead, the firstfruits of those who have fallen asleep.
1 Corinthians 15:20

The Feast of Pentecost was fulfilled through the indwelling of the Holy Spirit:

Do you not know that your body is a temple of the Holy Spirit, who is in you, whom you have received from God?
1 Corinthians 6:19

Similarly, the Feast Day of Trumpets will be fulfilled when Christ comes for his Bride, the Church, and awakens the dead in Christ with the final call of the *shofar*:

Listen, I tell you a mystery: We will not all sleep, but we will all be changed – in a flash, in the twinkling of an eye, at the last trumpet. *For the trumpet will sound, the dead will be raised imperishable, and we will be changed.*

1 Corinthians 15:51, 52

All of chapter 15 is within the context of Paul proclaiming the gospel and sequence of events to come:
Now, brothers, I want to remind you of the gospel I preached to you, which you received and on which you have taken your stand. By this gospel you are saved, if you hold firmly to the word I preached to you.

1 Corinthians 15:1-2

But Christ has indeed been raised from the dead, the firstfruits of those who have fallen asleep. For since death came through a man, the resurrection of the dead comes also through a man. For as in Adam all die, so in Christ all will be made alive. But each in his own turn: Christ, the firstfruits; then, when he comes, those who belong to him. Then the end will come, when he hands over the kingdom to God the Father after he has destroyed all dominion, authority and power. For he must reign until he has put all his enemies under his feet. The last enemy to be destroyed is death.

1 Corinthians 15:20-26

On the premise of the first four appointed feasts, not only should we actually expect the Feast Day of Trumpets to foreshadow the 'next event', but, armed with this knowledge from 1 Corinthians, especially chapter 15, we can discern that this is exactly what Paul believed too. As Paul preached the gospel, he evidently intertwined it with teaching about Christ's fulfilment of these prophecies from Leviticus.

In summary, we propose that just as surely as God precisely planned the former appointed feasts to have their fulfilment through Jesus Christ, so he has planned the next big event on his prophetic calendar, the Rapture of the Church, to be foreshadowed by the fifth appointed feast – the Day of Trumpets.

The Day of Atonement

The LORD said to Moses, 'The tenth day of this seventh month is the Day of Atonement. Hold a sacred assembly and deny yourselves, and present an offering made to the LORD by fire. Do no work on that day, because it is the Day of Atonement, when atonement is made for you before the LORD your God. Anyone who does not deny himself on that day must be cut off from his people. I will destroy from among his people anyone who does any work on that day. You shall do no work at all. This is to be a lasting ordinance for the generations to come, wherever you live. It is a sabbath of rest for you, and you must deny yourselves. From the evening of the ninth day of the month until the following evening you are to observe your sabbath.'

Leviticus 23:26-32

The objective of this Old Testament rationale has already been achieved through our analysis of the appointed Feast Day of Trumpets and its prophetic context. But while the subsequent two remaining appointed feasts of **Leviticus 23** foreshadow events which lie still further in the future, and hence are all the more open to speculation, we may see if anything can be learnt from them which may have a bearing on this chapter.

The sixth appointed celebration is called the Day of Atonement, or *Yom Kippur*. It occurs on tenth Tishrei, and is a very serious occasion in that it follows a week of repentance and soul-searching toward God after having celebrated the Day of Trumpets and Rosh Hashanah on 1st and 2nd Tishrei. During these days prayers are made for God to include one's name within the Book of Life for the coming year, and the Day of

Atonement marks the closing of that book and, in effect, the closing of the gates of Heaven through which such prayers are heard.

A special service is held on Yom Kippur called the Neilah, bringing an end to the opportunity for such prayers to enter through the 'open gates' of Heaven. From 1st Tishrei until 10th Tishrei these 10 days are known as the High Holy Days, or *Yomim Noraim,* such is their importance regarding a Jew's relationship with God, forgiveness, holiness, and place in Heaven.

It is at the end of the Neilah service, and hence the final act of this High Holy period which culminates with the awesome Day of Atonement, that another great shofar blast is given. While some have equated this to being the same type of blast given at the end of the Day of Trumpets, the *Tekiah Gedolah,* others have considered whether this blast might rightly be called the 'Great Shofar', in Hebrew the *Shofar Hagadol,* or the 'Great Trumpet'. The term *Shofar Hagadol* probably ought to be reserved as a special term referring to the great trumpet which accompanies the Messiah's glorious appearing.

In that day the LORD will thresh from the flowing Euphrates to the Wadi of Egypt, and you, O Israelites, will be gathered up one by one. And in that day a great trumpet will sound.

Isaiah 27:12-13

And he will send his angels with a loud trumpet call, and they will gather his elect from the four winds, from one end of the heavens to the other.

Matthew 24:31

However, in the context of our previous feasts and their prophetic relevance, it would come as no surprise whatsoever if the *Shofar Hagadol* were to be the prophetic fulfillment of the *shofar* blast given on the yearly Day of Atonement, as once this trumpet is sounded, the Book of Life is closed.

Please read through chapters eight and nine of the New Testament book of Hebrews. Within this passage we are reminded that the tabernacle and its contents, designed according to God's instructions, are but a copy of the real thing which exists in Heaven.

The point of what we are saying is this: We do have such a high priest, who sat down at the right hand of the throne of the Majesty in heaven, and who serves in the sanctuary, the true tabernacle set up by the Lord, not by man.
Every high priest is appointed to offer both gifts and sacrifices, and so it was necessary for this one also to have something to offer. If he were on earth, he would not be a priest, for there are already men who offer the gifts prescribed by the law. They serve at a sanctuary that is a copy and shadow of what is in Heaven. This is why Moses was warned when he was about to build the tabernacle: 'See to it that you make everything according to the pattern shown you on the mountain.'

Hebrews 8:1-5

While bearing this in mind, Hebrews also helpfully explains the relationship between the Old and New Covenants, and includes a summary of what the Day of Atonement was all about. In one atoning act of self-sacrifice Jesus has taken the place of the High Priest who would go into the Holy of Holies once per year on this day to offer animal's blood in atonement for Israel's sin.

For the life of a creature is in the blood, and I have given it to you to make atonement for yourselves on the altar; it is the blood that makes atonement for one's life.

Leviticus 17:11

When Christ came as high priest of the good things that are already here, he went through the greater and more perfect tabernacle that is not man-made, that is to say, not a part of this creation. He did not enter by means of the blood of goats and calves; but he entered the Most Holy Place once for all by his own blood, having obtained eternal redemption.

Hebrews 9:11, 12

The author of Hebrews is making it clear that just as the High Priest went into the Most Holy Place within the tabernacle on this most sacred Day of Atonement in order to offer the blood of sacrifices for the forgiveness of Israel's sin, so Jesus Christ had offered a sacrifice which is superior in every way. Through Christ's self-sacrifice, he has now entered the true Holy of Holies, which is in Heaven, to present himself before God in order that once and for all those who trust in him will be forgiven.

For this reason Christ is the mediator of a new covenant, that those who are called may receive the promised eternal inheritance – now that he has died as a ransom to set them free from the sins committed under the first covenant.

Hebrews 9:15

However, our question regarding this sixth appointed feast is whether, like the previous five feasts, it can be regarded as having a prophetic meaning of an event which has yet to be fulfilled. It is at this point that many of these clues come together to form a feasible proposal in this respect. Here is the evidence that this appointed day is a foreshadow of Jesus Christ's Glorious Appearing, otherwise known as his second coming.

It was necessary, then, for the copies of the heavenly things to be purified with these sacrifices, but the heavenly things themselves with better sacrifices than these. For Christ did not enter a man-made sanctuary that was only a copy of the true one; he entered Heaven itself, now to appear for us in God's presence. Nor did he enter Heaven to offer himself again and again, the way the high priest enters the Most Holy Place every year with blood that is not his own. Then Christ would have had to suffer many times since the creation of the world. But now he has appeared once for all at the end of the ages to do away with sin by the sacrifice of himself. Just as man is destined to die once, and after that to face judgment, so Christ was sacrificed once to take away the sins of many people; and he will appear a second time, not to bear sin, but to bring salvation to those who are waiting for him.

Hebrews 9:23-28

At the end of this lengthy passage within the book of Hebrews, which appears to go to great lengths to emphasise how much of the Old Covenant requirements foreshadow what was to come, we read in the last few verses of chapter nine a summary of what the author was trying to say with regard to the Day of Atonement. The author carefully explains the meaning and relevance behind this day and its requirements, and then states:

Just as man is destined to die once, and after that to face judgment, so Christ was sacrificed once to take away the sins of many people; and he will appear a second time, not to bear sin, but to bring salvation to those who are waiting for him.

Hebrews 9:27-28

There is a very direct connection being made between the Day of Atonement, its fulfilment in Heaven which has been accomplished, and then finally the Second Coming of this High Priest, this time '*to bring salvation to those who are waiting for him*'. When one considers the precise way in which the previous appointed feasts have been fulfilled we conclude that the Second Coming is possibly the prophetic fulfilment of the Day of Atonement. This argument is further enhanced by the very next verse after this reference to Christ's Second Coming:

105

The law is only a shadow of the good things that are coming - not the realities themselves.

Hebrews 10:1

Although this is speculation, it is nevertheless *calculated* speculation based upon our study of the previous appointed feasts. It would seem that just as the Passover, Feast of Unleavened Bread, Feasts of First Grain, Pentecost, and the Feast Day of Trumpets all have their prophetic reality of which they are a foreshadow, so the Day of Atonement includes much to suggest that it could foreshadow the great day when Christ shall return physically to earth to judge and to reign.

The first piece of evidence to support such speculation is the connection made by the writer of Hebrews between the Day of Atonement and the Second Coming. Given the precise detail contained within the letter it is most probable that the connection was intentional, if not assumed. It is immediately followed by that all-important verse which reminds us that the law, here referring to the Day of Atonement in particular, is *only a shadow of the good things that are coming*, in contrast to being a shadow of what Christ has already done. In other words, the Day of Atonement is a shadow of something that has yet to occur, and the only future event mentioned by the author of Hebrews in relation to this is the Second Coming, just one sentence beforehand.

The second piece of evidence is found in the blowing of the *shofar*. We have mentioned that this is blown as the final act of this awesome day, at the end of the Neilah service and at which time it is believed that the Book of Life is closed. How perfectly this fits as a prophecy of the Second Coming of Christ, at which time he will judge the living firstly according to their faith in him, and then according to their works for him, prior to reigning in the Millennial Kingdom. Certainly at that time the Book of

Life will be closed, and humankind will have had their opportunity to accept him as their Saviour, as now he comes as King of kings. Accompanying his Glorious Appearing, of course, is the sound of the *great trumpet*, not to be confused with any other, but the long awaited *Shofar Hagadol*, a wonderful fulfillment of the yearly *shofar* blast which ends this awesome day.

The final piece of evidence is the very nature of the Day of Atonement, remembering that it is the culmination of the 10 High Holy days, beginning with the Feast Day of Trumpets, which we already believe is a prophecy regarding the Rapture, and then a further seven days of introspection, repentance, and a turning toward God in humble prayer. The whole scenario reflects what we know about the pre-Tribulation Rapture being followed by seven years remaining for Israel to turn to God by recognising Jesus Christ as its Messiah. Seven years of judgment designed to facilitate the return of the Jews, reconciled to the Almighty through our one and only Saviour.

And I will pour out on the house of David and the inhabitants of Jerusalem a spirit of grace and supplication. They will look on me, the one they have pierced, and they will mourn for him as one mourns for an only child, and grieve bitterly for him as one grieves for a firstborn son.

Zechariah 12:10

These three pieces of evidence, when combined, have the ability to transform speculation into a credible possibility. If the Day of Atonement is indeed an appointed day which, like the other appointed feasts, is a prophecy regarding future events, then the evidence would indicate that it will find fulfilment in the Glorious Appearing of Jesus Christ. This is what the author of Hebrews described as being among the '*good things*' (**Hebrews 10:1**) which are to come.

The Feast of Tabernacles

The LORD said to Moses, 'Say to the Israelites: "On the fifteenth day of the seventh month the LORD's Feast of Tabernacles begins, and it lasts for seven days. The first day is a sacred assembly; do no regular work. For seven days present offerings made to the LORD by fire, and on the eighth day hold a sacred assembly and present an offering made to the LORD by fire. It is the closing assembly; do no regular work ... So beginning with the fifteenth day of the seventh month, after you have gathered the crops of the land, celebrate the festival to the LORD for seven days; the first day is a day of rest, and the eighth day also is a day of rest. On the first day you are to take choice fruit from the trees, and palm fronds, leafy branches and poplars, and rejoice before the LORD your God for seven days. Celebrate this as a festival to the LORD for seven days each year. This is to be a lasting ordinance for the generations to come; celebrate it in the seventh month. Live in booths for seven days: All native-born Israelites are to live in booths so your descendants will know that I had the Israelites live in booths when I brought them out of Egypt. I am the LORD your God."'

Leviticus 23:33-36, 38-44

The first five appointed feasts of Israel had a prophetic meaning which we can be sure of, while the Day of Atonement necessitated a degree of speculation, albeit quite persuasive.

The Feast of Tabernacles is the last of the appointed feasts, and accordingly if it has a prophetic meaning then we could expect it to foreshadow one of the very last events within God's story of salvation. At the same time, precisely because it has yet to be fulfilled, and is the furthest away in the prophetic calendar, we must acknowledge that any correlation between the Feast of Tabernacles and a future event will contain a yet larger degree of speculation and uncertainty. Therefore, we shall keep this part of the proposal brief.

The Feast of Tabernacles is also known as Sukkot, or the Festival of Booths. It begins on 15th day of the seventh month, Tishrei, with a Sabbath day, then lasts for seven days, and then on the eighth day another Sabbath is observed.

As the text from Leviticus suggests, it marked the final harvest of the year. It was a celebration which was eagerly anticipated following the seriousness of the Day of Atonement. The idea of living in temporary tabernacles, booths or tents during this time was a reminder that the Lord is God, that he alone rescued them from the slavery of Egypt, looked after them in the wilderness, and brought them to the promised land. Ultimately God alone was, and is, their Provider.

The seventh of these important days is called *Hoshana Rabba*, which means 'Great Salvation', and it completes the entire period from the Feast Day of Trumpets, through the High Holy Days and the Day of Atonement, up to the end of the Feast of Tabernacles. This whole period is considered to be the period of Divine Judgment. The Feast culminates with a final Sabbath.

The most natural conclusion for those who recognise the prophetic nature of the previous six feasts, would be to suggest that the Feast of Tabernacles foreshadows the Millennial Kingdom of **Revelation 20:1-6**. Not only does the 1,000 year reign of Christ on earth once again demonstrate the perfect provision of God, but its end will also complete the future period of divine judgment, which begins at the Rapture when the Church is taken to Heaven.

Similar to this Feast's end of harvest celebrations, the Millennial Kingdom begins after the final harvest of souls, at the end of the Tribulation, when Christ returns gloriously to defeat those who oppose him and to separate the 'sheep' from the 'goats'. At the end of the 1,000 years there is a final judgment which ushers in the new Heaven and new earth (**Revelation 21:1-5**) in which those who have placed their trust in Christ for their salvation will live for eternity. The last day then, certainly is a day of *Hoshana Rabba* – Great Salvation!

Perhaps the greatest argument for the Feast of Tabernacles to be not only a lasting ordinance for the Jews since the time of Moses, but also a prophecy of God's perfect plan of salvation, is found by reading the words of the Old Testament prophet Zechariah. Having described the world conditions and Israel's place in it prior to the Glorious Appearing of the Messiah, he then provides a glimpse of what the 1,000 year reign of Christ will be like. This goes hand-in-hand with our references to Revelation, but it makes specific reference to the importance at that time of the Feast of Tabernacles. As this Feast is the only one to get a mention, one may speculate that the Millennial Kingdom is, indeed, the fulfillment of this appointed feast.

On that day his feet will stand on the Mount of Olives, east of Jerusalem, and the Mount of Olives will be split in two from east to west, forming a great valley, with half of the mountain moving north and half moving south. You will flee by my mountain valley, for it will extend to Azel. You will flee as you fled from the earthquake in the days of Uzziah king of Judah. Then the LORD my God will come, and all the holy ones with him.
On that day there will be no light, no cold or frost. It will be a unique day, without daytime or nighttime – a day known to the LORD. When evening comes, there will be light.
On that day living water will flow out from Jerusalem, half to the eastern sea and half to the western sea, in summer and in winter. The LORD will be king over the whole earth. On that day there will be one LORD, and his name the only name …
Then the survivors from all the nations that have attacked Jerusalem will go up year after year to worship the King, the LORD Almighty, and to celebrate the Feast of Tabernacles. If any of the peoples of the earth do not go up to Jerusalem to worship the King,

the LORD Almighty, they will have no rain. If the Egyptian people do not go up and take part, they will have no rain. The LORD will bring on them the plague he inflicts on the nations that do not go up to celebrate the Feast of Tabernacles. This will be the punishment of Egypt and the punishment of all the nations that do not go up to celebrate the Feast of Tabernacles.

Zechariah 14:4-9, 16-19

Conclusion

So Moses announced to the Israelites the appointed feasts of the LORD.

Leviticus 23:44

Our spiritual life, relationship with God and attitude toward Scripture is enhanced if we keep in mind that God's Word is intrinsically Jewish. It is true that non-Jews are also able to take advantage of the availability of salvation to the whosoever, freely offered by grace through faith alone in Jesus Christ. However, it is important to remember that the Old Testament was written by Jews, for Jews, and that God certainly has not forgotten nor broken his promise to his Jewish people. This means, in turn, that we can learn so much about our Christian faith if only we would consider its Jewish roots, and the Jewish context on which our faith is built.

Not only, then, are we called to bless Israel (**Genesis 12:1-3**), but we can learn so much from the Jewish faith and traditions too. This chapter has merely demonstrated how the passage of Leviticus 23, which may at first appear so exclusive to Jews, is actually an incredible manuscript of past and future events. They were foretold by God to his servant Moses, and recorded for the benefit of the Jews as acts of remembrance, celebration and worship. But they are also invaluable to every believer as prophecies of events which had to be fulfilled by the Jewish Messiah, Jesus Christ.

Without Christ, these feasts are void of relevance to the non-Jew. But with Christ, they become packed with meaning and purpose to Jew and Gentile alike.

It is evident that the Passover, Feast of Unleavened Bread, Feast of First Grain, and Pentecost, which are the first four appointed feasts of Leviticus 23, also had the purpose of prophesying the gospel of Christ. They have been fulfilled by Jesus Christ through his sacrificial death, victory over sin, resurrection, and gift of the Holy Spirit respectively. In this study we have shown this to be true and it would be negligent for us not to believe that the remaining three feasts had a similarly prophetic purpose.

While the final two feasts have parallels with eschatological teaching about the Glorious Appearing of Christ and his rule within the Millennial Kingdom culminating in the final judgment, the focus of this Old Testament rationale has been on that fifth feast, the Day of Trumpets.

Just as the first four feasts have an undeniable prophetic quality about events which Christ fulfilled in the past, so the Feast Day of Trumpets can be assumed to have a prophetic purpose. It would make most sense for this special day to relate to the 'next event' on God's prophetic calendar, and it certainly has a very strong argument for being the foreshadow of the pre-Tribulation Rapture of the Church.

Other biblical considerations

In the previous two chapters we have studied a New Testament rationale for the pre-Tribulation Rapture concept, and also an Old Testament rationale based on the seven appointed feasts of Leviticus 23. The first of these rationales carries a great deal of weight. It is persuasive. The second rationale is less persuasive by itself, but is nevertheless a useful confirmation of the futurist interpretation of Revelation, and certainly adds weight to the Rapture concept while demonstrating the sovereignty of God.

Once we put these two rationales together their evidence becomes all the more potent. The Rapture concept is by no means obscure, but merely requires deliberate study and understanding. It has its similarities to the doctrine of the Trinity in that, without being specifically mentioned, it is evident that the Bible teaches these truths, and indeed in many cases assumes that they are true.

In this chapter we shall endeavour to add yet more weight to the pre-Tribulation Rapture concept, not by lengthy arguments, but by drawing upon a series of seven complementary lines of reasoning which are based purely on Scripture. In addition we shall consider a few of the more common responses to a pre-Tribulation viewpoint, followed by a further seven considerations.

1 The disappearance of the Church

There is a very persuasive line of reasoning for a pre-Tribulation Rapture which often gets relegated to being an 'additional' or 'complementary' piece of evidence for two reasons: firstly, because it may be classed as an oversimplified view of Revelation, and secondly, because there is a chance that this argument is coincidental. Nevertheless, it is most certainly worthy of mention, even as the first among our *'other biblical considerations'*. It really is quite staggering in itself, and certainly adds a significant amount of support to the pre-Tribulation Rapture concept.

Within the first three chapters of the book of Revelation the Church is referred to nearly 20 times, either specifically or generally. The Church features predominantly.

Chapters four and five then describe John's vision of what is taking place in Heaven immediately prior to the opening of the first seal of judgment, and then chapters six to 19 of Revelation describe the seven years of Tribulation. Within these 14 chapters we have descriptions of all the key 'characters' in this end-time scenario. They include the antichrist's rise to power, the false prophet who supports him, the judgments of God, and the re-emergence of Israel as the pride and people of God who turn to Jesus and are persecuted as a result, culminating in the Glorious Appearing.

In these 14 chapters which dominate the book we have general descriptions as well as detailed accounts. The Tribulation, Israel's final seven years from the 70 'weeks' of years which Daniel foresaw (**Daniel 9:24-27**), simply cannot begin to be understood until **Revelation 6-19** is brought into the study.

But the Church has disappeared. In fact the words 'church' and 'churches' do not occur even once within this lengthy passage. An immediate conclusion must surely be that the Church is not mentioned during this most detailed account of the Tribulation for the obvious reason that the Church as we know it simply is not there. After having been mentioned and referred to nearly 20 times within the first three chapters, the Church is absent from these vital 14 chapters which focus on the Tribulation. It has been *'caught up'* in a pre-Tribulation Rapture.

There are two main objections to this observation. The first is that the term *'saints'* is found within the Tribulation chapters as referring to believers in Christ (for example **Revelation 13:7, 10; 14:12; 16:6; 17:6**). The point remains, however, that for some reason these believers have suddenly stopped being identified as the Church, and so it would appear that those who come to Christ *after the start* of the Tribulation are called 'saints' in order to distinguish them from those who believed before. Otherwise we are at a loss to explain the change in terminology.

Indeed, one of the references to these 'saints' also serves to distinguish them from the Church.

He was given power to make war against the saints and to conquer them.

Revelation 13:7

As this verse is talking about the antichrist we know that the saints are those who believe *after* the antichrist has risen to power. Furthermore, by comparing this verse with Jesus' promise concerning the Church we remain convinced that these Tribulation saints are those who become Christians after the Rapture.

"And I tell you that you are Peter, and on this rock I will build my church, and the gates of Hades will not overcome it. I will give you the keys of the kingdom of Heaven; whatever you bind on earth will be bound in Heaven, and whatever you loose on earth will be loosed in Heaven."

Matthew 16:18, 19

Quite clearly the above two texts cannot be referring to the same group of believers.

The second objection comes in that the word 'churches' does occur *after* the Tribulation passage.

115

'I, Jesus, have sent my angel to give you this testimony for the churches.'

Revelation 22:16

However, it is plain to see that this reference occurs not only after the Tribulation chapters of 6-19, but is even at the very end of Revelation, upon completion of the vision, where Jesus tells John that this prophetic book has been given for our benefit. Therefore, rather than damaging our argument, it actually further confirms it by drawing attention to the absence of the Church in the intervening chapters.

In summary, following the vision's initial focus on the Church within the first three chapters of Revelation, we have a situation where the focus is switched to the seven-year Tribulation, and in the entire 14 chapters the Church is not mentioned once. It is mysteriously omitted from this section which is concerned with Israel's final seven years. It is not present on earth during the years of God's wrath. It has been *'caught up'* in a pre-Tribulation Rapture.

2 The Rapture of John

After this I looked, and there before me was a door standing open in Heaven. And the voice I had first heard speaking to me like a trumpet said. 'Come up here, and I will show you what must take place after this.'

Revelation 4:1

This verse, which acts as a bridge between the message to the churches and events in Heaven prior to the Tribulation, has striking similarities to the Rapture concept's key texts.

John, who many believe was the 'beloved disciple' within the Gospel accounts (***John 13:23; 20:2; 21:7, 20***), may here be a

representative of the Church, the Body of Christ, or beloved of
Christ.

*Husbands, love your wives, just as Christ loved the Church and
gave himself up for her to make her holy, cleansing her by the
washing with water through the word, and to present her to
himself as a radiant Church, without stain or wrinkle or any other
blemish, but holy and blameless.*

Ephesians 5:25-27

The whole passage from Paul's letter to the **Ephesians 5:21-33**
speaks not only about the relationship between husband and wife,
but also between Christ and his Church. If, then, Christ's beloved
disciple John is representative of the Church, then just as
Revelation 4:1 describes John's translation to Heaven, so it may
well prophesy the Rapture of the Church.

Certainly there is plenty of evidence to help substantiate this. First
of all, John hears the voice *'like a trumpet'*, which has its obvious
similarities to the key Rapture texts of **1 Thessalonians 4:16** and
1 Corinthians 15:52. Secondly John is responding to Jesus' voice,
telling him to *'come up here'*, and he enters through an *'open
door'*. These terms not only fit our knowledge and description of
the Rapture but they were also previously used by Jesus and
recorded by John. Jesus is the gate, while John represents the
sheep who respond to his voice.

*'I am the good shepherd; I know my sheep and my sheep know me
– just as the Father knows me and I know the Father – and I lay
down my life for the sheep. I have other sheep that are not of this
sheep pen. I must bring them also. They too will listen to my voice,
and there shall be one flock and one shepherd.*

John 10:14-16

*Therefore Jesus said again, 'I tell you the truth, I am the gate for
the sheep. All who ever came before me were thieves and robbers,*

but the sheep did not listen to them. I am the gate; whoever enters through me will be saved.'

John 10:7-9

However, the third and strongest piece of evidence to link ***Revelation 4:1*** with a future, pre-Tribulation Rapture is the fact that it occurs after all the many references to the Church, and before the start of the references to the Tribulation. In fact, it marks the point when the Church disappears from the script.

It occurs precisely at the time one would expect it to from the perspective of the pre-Tribulation Rapture theory. The final two words of this verse are incredibly informative for this purpose.

After this I looked, and there before me was a door standing open in Heaven. And the voice I had first heard speaking to me like a trumpet said, 'Come up here, and I will show you what must take place after this.'

Revelation 4:1

The last two words, *'after this'* clearly refer to what has gone on before (the letters to the churches) and what will happen immediately afterward (the Tribulation). ***Revelation 4:1***, then, not only appears to be an account describing the Rapture of John, but it seems to be included at a particularly convenient part of the vision which gives it stunning parallels with the pre-Tribulation Rapture concept.

3 Those who live in Heaven

The beast was given a mouth to utter proud words and blasphemies and to exercise his authority for forty-two months. He opened his mouth to blaspheme God, and to slander his name and his dwelling place and those who live in Heaven. He was given

*power to make war against the saints and to conquer them. And
he was given authority over every tribe, people, language and
nation. All inhabitants of the earth will worship the beast – all
whose names have not been written in the book of life belonging to
the Lamb that was slain from the creation of the world.*

Revelation 13:5-8

This passage describes the actions of the Antichrist halfway
through the seven-year period, when his hatred and persecution
of true believers will intensify. This is when he will also be
recognised by the Jews as a deceiver as he sets up the
abomination in the Temple at this three-and-a-half-year point.
These actions also disclose the status of the Church, and
subsequent Christians. We read how he blasphemes God, and
how he slanders God's name, his dwelling place, as well as *'those
who live in Heaven'*.

His blasphemy is, of course, the signal for the Jews to recognise
Christ as their Messiah, and his slander of God and Heaven would
naturally follow for anyone who was claiming to discredit Judaism
and Christianity.

However, the particularly interesting thing to note is that he also
slanders *'those who live in Heaven'*. Now if the resurrection and
Rapture (which we know from our key texts will occur hand in
hand) have not yet taken place, then it is difficult to see who
these inhabitants of Heaven could possibly be. In addition, there
would be very little, if any, gain to be made by slandering those
who live in Heaven if they are unknown to those on earth.

It makes far more logical sense, then, to assume that the antichrist
slanders those who live in Heaven because they *used* to be on
earth, and indeed because of their relationship with the God
about whom he is blaspheming. *'Those who live in Heaven'*, then,
can only refer to those who have been caught up in the Rapture.

119

In the Church's absence it would be easy to slander those who have gone to Heaven, not only because of little remaining resistance to such words, but also because of the possible mayhem and grief that may have immediately ensued.

This would suggest that God and *'those who live in Heaven'* will be slandered because the Rapture has occurred. Popularity ratings will not matter, for the antichrist is also able to get away with saying such things about God because the Rapture has occurred. Indeed, his emergence to power is unhindered precisely because the Church is not here, they are living in Heaven. The Rapture has already occurred!

4 The Lord knows how to rescue the godly from trials

For if God did not spare angels when they sinned, but sent them to hell, putting them into gloomy dungeons to be held for judgment; if he did not spare the ancient world when he brought the flood on its ungodly people, but protected Noah, a preacher of righteousness, and seven others; if he condemned the cities of Sodom and Gomorrah by burning them to ashes, and made them an example of what is going to happen to the ungodly; and if he rescued Lot, a righteous man, who was distressed by the filthy lives of lawless men (for that righteous man, living among them day after day, was tormented in his righteous soul by the lawless deeds he saw and heard) – if this is so, then the Lord knows how to rescue godly men from trials and to hold the unrighteous for the day of judgment, while continuing their punishment.

2 Peter 2:4-9

In attempting to understand Peter's words, this fourth consideration would suggest that this passage not only illustrates how God tends to keep his people protected from his wrath, but may also be a specific reference to the future wrath of the

Tribulation. Either way, the Lord knows how to rescue the godly from trials, and a pre-Tribulation Rapture would be perfectly in keeping with his previous acts of provision.

5 God has not finished with the Jews

God did not reject his people, whom he foreknew ...
Again I ask: did they stumble so as to fall beyond recovery? Not at all! Rather, because of their transgression, salvation has come to the Gentiles to make Israel envious. But if their transgression means riches for the world, and their loss means riches for the Gentiles, how much greater riches will their fullness bring!

Romans 11:2, 11, 12

This study has already made mention of this truth on several occasions, and is a biblical precept for understanding scriptural eschatology. In particular we have examined Daniel's prophecy regarding a final 'week' of years yet to be fulfilled by Israel (**Daniel 9:24-27**), and how those seven years constitute the period known as the Tribulation (**Matthew 24:15-25**).

It is during this period that 144,000 Jewish missionaries receive the seal of the living God, 12,000 from each tribe (**Revelation 7:1-14**), whose zeal produces a great multitude of believers in Jesus Christ. We know that their efforts are made in Christ's name because the converted have *'have washed their robes and made them white in the blood of the Lamb' (**Revelation 7:14**)*. Perhaps the readiness of these Jews to evangelise is spurred on by the preceding Rapture. That would be speculation, but certainly we have evidence from history that once Jews become acquainted with Christ as their Messiah then their missionary enthusiasm is unmatched.

We may legitimately ask, then, where the Church is during this time. The purpose of this book is to investigate the proposal that it has already been caught up to Heaven through the Rapture. The New Testament letter from Paul to the Romans is perhaps the best explanation regarding the relationship between God, the times of the Gentiles which includes the Church age, and the fulfilment of Israel's 70 weeks of years.

Romans chapter 11 is a vital read, though the preceding few chapters would provide a worthwhile and fuller context. In this section of the letter Paul is careful to encourage his Gentile readers not to boast of their new-found spiritual status at the expense of the Jews, and he writes this for two precise reasons.

Firstly, he reminds the Gentile Christians that their faith has its roots in Judaism, and indeed could not exist had it not been for God's chosen race, the Jews. This in itself should be good enough reason not to boast over, or care less for Israel.

If the part of the dough offered as firstfruits is holy, then the whole batch is holy; if the root is holy, so are the branches.
If some of the branches have been broken off, and you, though a wild olive shoot, have been grafted in among the others and now share in the nourishing sap from the olive root, do not boast over those branches. If you do, consider this: you do not support the root, but the root supports you.

Romans 11:16-18

Secondly, Paul teaches the Gentile Christians that just as they have been adopted into God's family through faith in the Jewish Messiah, Jesus Christ, so they must recognise that it would be logical for the natural children of God to be welcomed back into the family – again only through faith in Jesus Christ.

You will say then, 'Branches were broken off so that I could be grafted in.' Granted. But they were broken off because of unbelief, and you stand by faith ... And if they do not persist in unbelief, they will be grafted in, for God is able to graft them in again. After all, if you were cut out of an olive tree that is wild by nature, and contrary to nature were grafted into a cultivated olive tree, how much more readily will these, the natural branches, be grafted into their own olive tree!

Romans 11:19-20, 23-24

During the final seven years allotted to Israel, God's chosen race will indeed be grafted back in.

I do not want you to be ignorant of this mystery, brothers, so that you may not be conceited: Israel has experienced a hardening in part until the full number of the Gentiles has come in. And so all Israel will be saved, as it is written.

Romans 11:25, 26

Once again this whole theme of Israel returning to God through Jesus Christ is further support of a pre-Tribulation concept, in which the Church is caught up to Heaven prior to Israel's final seven years. Indeed the last of the above texts clearly implies that the *'hardening'* of Israel is only temporary, and that once the Church age, or times of the Gentiles, has been completed, then Israel will recognise the Messiah Jesus and be saved.

6 The Bride of Christ

One of the seven angels who had the seven bowls full of the seven last plagues came and said to me, 'Come, I will show you the bride, the wife of the Lamb.' And he carried me away in the Spirit to a mountain great and high, and showed me the Holy City, Jerusalem, coming down out of Heaven from God. It shone with the glory of God, and its brilliance was like that of a very precious jewel, like a jasper, clear as crystal. It had a great, high wall with twelve gates, and with twelve angels at the gates. On the gates were written the names of the twelve tribes of Israel. There were three gates on the east, three on the north, three on the south and three on the west. The wall of the city had twelve foundations, and on them were the names of the twelve apostles of the Lamb.

Revelation 21:9-14

The Church is often referred to as being the Bride or Wife of Christ (for example ***John 3:29; Revelation 19:7; Ephesians 5:21-33; 2 Corinthians 11:2***). In the text above we also read of the city of God, our future eternal dwelling, being described as '*the bride, the wife of the Lamb*'. Just as buildings today are sometimes called churches, and yet any church, and especially the universal Church, is comprised of the people rather than the material, so this city is called the Bride because it is the 'building' or environment which we shall one day occupy.

A deeper study would reveal interesting links between the Jewish customs surrounding marriage in Jesus' day and the sequence of events according to a pre-Tribulation Rapture concept. Such a study might suggest that the idea of marriage between Jesus and the Church is similar to those Jewish weddings (for example ***Matthew 1:18-25***). It consists of a betrothal, preparing the future accommodation, then, at the father's discretion, the groom collects the bride and takes her home, consummates the marriage over a period of one week before celebrating with friends at a feast or marriage supper. The respective parallels would be our salvation upon trusting in Christ's atoning work (***John 3:16, 17***), Christ going to prepare a place for the Church in Heaven (***John 14:2, 3***), then, at the Father's timing (***Mark 13:32***) coming to collect the Church at the Rapture (***1 Thessalonians 4:16, 17***), and after the week of Israel's years celebrating the marriage supper of the Lamb (***Revelation 19:9***).

However significant these parallels may be, what is of particular interest is the fact that all references to the 'Bride' or the 'Wife of the Lamb' within **Revelation 19-21** clearly reveal that she is not to be found on earth, but is in Heaven with God until he comes down with her to reign on earth. These same references infer that the Bride of Christ, the Church, has been in Heaven awaiting this moment, and therefore must have previously been caught up in the Rapture.

Then I saw a new Heaven and a new earth, for the first Heaven and the first earth had passed away, and there was no longer any sea. I saw the Holy City, the new Jerusalem, coming down out of Heaven from God, prepared as a bride beautifully dressed for her husband. And I heard a loud voice from the throne saying, 'Now the dwelling of God is with men, and he will live with them. They will be his people, and God himself will be with them and be their God. He will wipe every tear from their eyes. There will be no more death or mourning or crying or pain, for the old order of things has passed away.'
He who was seated on the throne said, 'I am making everything new!' Then he said, 'Write this down, for these words are trustworthy and true.'

Revelation 21:1-5

7 An unknown season

Therefore keep watch, because you do not know on what day your Lord will come. But understand this: If the owner of the house had known at what time of night the thief was coming, he would have kept watch and would not have let his house be broken into. So you also must be ready, because the Son of Man will come at an hour when you do not expect him.

Matthew 24:44

The above text makes it clear that we cannot know for sure when Jesus Christ will come for us. We have already shown how this contrasts with our knowledge that the Glorious Appearing must take place seven years after the confirmation of a covenant involving Israel, or three and a half years after the abomination is set up in the Temple (**Daniel 9:27**). Therefore Christ must be coming for his Church prior to these seven years in order for it to be at an *unknown* time.

However, these verses emphasise the point that it is not merely the *day* which is unknown, but it is the *season* which is unknown. **Matthew 24:44** says that he will come at an *hour* when we do not expect him. Of course, given that the Gospel author had just told us that the *day* is unknown, it would make little sense for him to say that the actual hour (60 minutes) is unknown. Instead, it is reasonable to deduce that the word 'hour' refers to a time, a season, and a general climate. This would be in accord with all other similar texts. Including **Acts 1:7:**
He said to them: 'It is not for you to know the times or dates the Father has set by his own authority.'

If we compare this unknown *hour* to **Luke 21:28,** where the end of the Tribulation is described, we can ascertain that they are quite different events: *'When these things begin to take place, stand up and lift up your heads, because your redemption is drawing near.'*

The difference is vital. The second coming is to be looked for, while Christ's coming for the Church will come suddenly. The fact that it is not merely the day which is unknown but the wider time frame too adds yet more credibility to the belief that this Rapture will occur prior to the Tribulation.

Resolving potential difficulties

Matthew 24-25 is at once a vital and yet complex ingredient to Scriptural eschatology. It would be good for the reader to read these two chapters, as well as **Mark 13**.

Some of the most common objections to the pre-Tribulation Rapture concept arise through disagreement about whether Jesus was talking about the Rapture or about his second coming to judge all nations. This is especially true when at times they seem to be mentioned in extremely close proximity to each other within the text, such as occurs within these chapters.

We can demonstrate the need for this vital separation of end-time events by taking a look at the following text.

When the Son of Man comes in his glory, and all the angels with him, he will sit on his throne in heavenly glory. All the nations will be gathered before him, and he will separate the people one from another as a shepherd separates the sheep from the goats. He will put the sheep on his right and the goats on his left.
Matthew 25:31-33

This is sometimes referred to as being the 'next event' by those unfamiliar with biblical eschatology. However, within the framework of the end-times this text needs to be discounted as such because it actually refers to a post-Tribulation judgement. This is not the same event as Jesus describes in our Rapture texts, such as in **Matthew 24:36-44,** despite its close proximity. There are immense differences which indicate that this is not talking about the Rapture but his second coming, that is his Glorious Appearing.

Firstly, the passage's context is one of judgment. The unrighteous 'goats' are sent to eternal punishment, the righteous 'sheep' to eternal life. This judgment of unbelievers does not coincide with any Rapture texts, but if anything the Rapture would provide an extended opportunity for them to prioritise their spiritual relationship with God.

Furthermore, the very manner in which these people are being separated is completely different. In this text Jesus describes the nations being brought before him as King, whereas the Rapture texts refer to Jesus separating believers from unbelievers in an instant, unexpectedly, while they are still at work even, and transforming their bodies into glorious ones as quick as a flash (*1 Corinthians 15:51, 52*). While this passage describes the Son of Man coming in his glory, and unbelievers anticipating their judgment (and even calling him Lord, **Matthew 25:44**), the passages describing the Rapture teach believers to keep watch in case we are taken by surprise, while unbelievers will be completely unaware.

This may seem straightforward at first, but as these and other important chapters are read, the matter can become somewhat confusing, especially if the passages are smaller and regularly alternating between accounts of the Rapture, Tribulation, Glorious Appearing and Judgment. However, while recognising this as a minor inconvenience, we also need to recognise this style of writing is both legitimate and even expected.

This notion of having to sort through these texts carefully to examine whether they refer to one event or another may not be consistent with modern narrations today. However, this was exactly what the prophet Isaiah did on a regular basis regarding the coming of the Messiah. Not only did this cause similar problems of needing to sort through the material, but it even caused some to miss the truth that the Messiah would come in humility prior to coming in glory.

A voice of one calling: 'In the desert prepare the way for the LORD; make straight in the wilderness a highway for our God.
Every valley shall be raised up, every mountain and hill made low; the rough ground shall become level, the rugged places a plain.
And the glory of the LORD will be revealed, and all mankind together will see it. For the mouth of the LORD has spoken.'
Isaiah 40:3-5

This particular example illustrates how Isaiah would almost be referring to two things at once, prophesying the mission of John the Baptist in verse three, but prophesying the end-time in verses four and five. With hindsight, it is much easier to understand this method of interpretation.

For to us a child is born, to us a son is given, and the government will be on his shoulders.
And he will be called Wonderful Counselor, Mighty God, Everlasting Father, Prince of Peace.
Of the increase of his government and peace there will be no end. He will reign on David's throne and over his kingdom, establishing and upholding it with justice and righteousness from that time on and forever.
The zeal of the LORD Almighty will accomplish this.

Isaiah 9:6-7

Similarly, in Isaiah 9:6, 7 we have Christ coming as a baby, and Christ coming as the Prince of Peace, one verse after another, without interruption, clearly referring to the same person, and yet we now equally clearly know that these verses are prophesying events that will be more than 2,000 years apart.

The point is that this form of writing, particularly with regard to prophecy, was abundant in the Old Testament. This has two clear lessons for us within our study. Firstly it reassures us that to propose that Scripture teaches that Christ will come for his Church *prior* to his Glorious Appearing is perfectly acceptable if the evidence is there. Secondly, we recognise that passages such as Matthew 24, 25 include precisely this same sort of dual-referencing such as Isaiah used. This should be no surprise as Matthew often used Isaiah's writings.

So let us consider some potential areas of confusion and attempt to clarify some more end-time texts which may otherwise provoke doubt on the pre-Tribulation Rapture.

1 Who are 'the elect'?

At that time the sign of the Son of Man will appear in the sky, and all the nations of the earth will mourn. They will see the Son of Man coming on the clouds of the sky, with power and great glory. And he will send his angels with a loud trumpet call, and they will gather his elect from the four winds, from one end of the heavens to the other.

Matthew 24:30, 31

This passage is clearly referring to the Glorious Appearing as everyone will see Christ. This will occur at the end of the Tribulation. However, some have argued that the presence of the '*elect*' along with the '*trumpet call*' provides proof that the Church is not caught up to be with Christ until he comes on the clouds to judge the earth. This is an argument made by proponents of a post-Tribulation Rapture.

In response, we need to firstly clarify that, as mentioned in a previous chapter, the '*loud trumpet call*' is the *Shofar Hagadol* of **Isaiah 27:13**, and as such is not likely to be that which we have already associated with the Rapture, the *Tekiah Gedolah*. Even without getting into such detail we can quickly decipher that there are many trumpet references within Scripture, in conjunction with the end-time, and at the very least we need to be wary of interpreting this text as being associated with our key Rapture texts merely on the basis of a trumpet call. It would be as speculative as making similar connections with texts that refer to angels or clouds.

With regard to the '*elect*', the same term is used to describe God's chosen people in verses 22 and 24, as they encounter the miraculous signs which will be performed by the false prophets within the future time of distress. I believe '*the elect*' are those who have not been caught up in the pre-Tribulation Rapture, but

130

through the subsequent seven years will turn to God through Jesus Christ. It may even be worth considering that the *'elect'* are exactly that, an elected number of people, chosen by God for a specific purpose. This line of reasoning is speculative, but it would certainly tie in with the knowledge we have that there are indeed four angels who are associated with an elected number of Jews within the Tribulation period.

After this I saw four angels standing at the four corners of the earth, holding back the four winds of the earth to prevent any wind from blowing on the land or on the sea or on any tree. Then I saw another angel coming up from the east, having the seal of the living God. He called out in a loud voice to the four angels who had been given power to harm the land and the sea: 'Do not harm the land or the sea or the trees until we put a seal on the foreheads of the servants of our God.' Then I heard the number of those who were sealed: 144,000 from all the tribes of Israel.

Revelation 7:1-4

In putting these two passages together, we could easily conclude that *'the elect'* are God's chosen people, his elect, saved, and servant Jews who will be sealed before the four angels release the four winds to harm the earth, and who will likewise be gathered, possibly by the same four angels, at Christ's Glorious Appearing.

Finally, it may also be worth noting that in this passage it is the *angels* who gather the elect, whereas these gathering angels are noticeably absent from our key Rapture texts, and instead our passages in *John 14:3* and *1 Thessalonians 4:16* make the contrast in asserting it is the Lord himself who will take the Church to be with him.

Rather than produce a difficulty, then, this record of Jesus' end-time prophecy from *Matthew 24:30, 31* might actually provide us with further confirmation that our futurist interpretation of Revelation is valid, and that the Church will be caught up in a pre-Tribulation Rapture.

2 The Last Day?

And this is the will of him who sent me, that I shall lose none of all that he has given me, but raise them up at the last day.

John 6:39

No one can come to me unless the Father who sent me draws him, and I will raise him up at the last day.

John 6:44

Whoever eats my flesh and drinks my blood has eternal life, and I will raise him up at the last day.

John 6:54

Martha answered, 'I know he will rise again in the resurrection at the last day.'

John 11:24

'There is a judge for the one who rejects me and does not accept my words; that very word which I spoke will condemn him at the last day.'

John 12:48

The term 'the last day' is evidently closely related to the day of resurrection, and therefore to the Rapture. If we are correct in our belief in a pre-Tribulation Rapture we need to respond to other ideas based on these verses. These ideas are that the resurrection and Rapture will not take place until the very last day, meaning the very last 24-hour period before there is a new Heaven, a new earth, in which there will be no more night and, by implication, no separation of night and day.

There will be no more night. They will not need the light of a lamp or the light of the sun, for the Lord God will give them light. And they will reign for ever and ever.

Revelation 22:5

This is a popular argument used by proponents of post-Tribulation Rapture. At first glance the continual repetition of those words found in John's Gospel, '*the last day*', may make us think it is a powerful and convincing defence of such a position. However, as we examine these phrases we can determine that this argument is far weaker than it might at first seem.

We may respond by reminding ourselves that our study of the '*last trumpet*' of **1 Corinthians 15:52** included the recognition that Paul probably did not mean the last trumpet *of any kind and forever*, but was referring to a specific trumpet call, which was the last in a series, as well as being the last trumpet for the Church. Similarly, though '*the last day*' may literally mean the final 24-hours before Heaven, this cannot be assumed, and needs to be affirmed by other Scripture. However, there is no supporting Scripture.

Indeed, we could just as easily say that '*the last day*' refers to *our* last day on earth, that it occurs with and includes '*the last trumpet*', and that both refer to the pre-Tribulation Rapture itself occurring on the last day of the Church age.

It seems odd that in each of these verses from John listed above, he records Jesus as having said '*at* the last day'. This seems to indicate a different meaning to something which may occur '*on* the last day'. If he intended to say that he would raise everyone at one moment on the very last day before Heaven is enjoyed, then it would have been natural to say that the resurrection would occur '*on* the last day'. Indeed, this is how the Gospel author spoke of the very last day of the Feast of Tabernacles.

On the last and greatest day of the Feast, Jesus stood and said in a loud voice, 'If anyone is thirsty, let him come to me and drink.'

John 7:37

Here, the phrase *'on the last and greatest day'* is used, clearly indicating it is the *very* last day of the Feast which is meant. This is a notable difference from saying *'at the last'*, despite being within the same Gospel, and in the middle of the above six texts under examination.

The very fact that Jesus made such a difference would indicate that his phrase *'at the last day'* may mean something other than the final 24-hour period. This suggestion, along with the above texts, may lead us instead to believe that *'at the last day'* refers to when Christ shall return at his Glorious Appearing. This is the time when the Tribulation saints shall be resurrected and will reign with Christ (**Revelation 20:4-5**). Alternatively it may equally refer to *'the last day'* for Christians, synonymous with the day of the Rapture, when we know the Church will be resurrected and caught up together (**1 Corinthians 15:50-54**).

Either way, in the account of raising Lazarus in **John 11**, Jesus proved that whenever the last day is believed to be, he has the authority and power to resurrect people by merely calling them from the grave. This is true whether that is now, at the Rapture, or at his Glorious Appearing. Even if *'the last day'* refers to his Glorious Appearing, this may not be a reason to discount a prior resurrection at the Rapture.

On the subject of interpretation, it should also be noted that proponents of this view not only tend to adhere to the post-Tribulation Rapture idea, but also are split on the issue of the Millennial Kingdom. A belief that Jesus was referring to the last 24 hours before our eternity in Heaven must either lead to a belief that this 'day' occurs at the end of Christ's thousand-year reign

(**Revelation 20:1-7**) or that no such Millennial Kingdom will exist, so that there can be no subsequent 'days'. Either way causes problems with regard to interpreting other passages of biblical eschatology.

For example, if the 'day' of resurrection and Rapture is the very last of the thousand years, then we are unable to identify who accompanies Christ when he defeats the antichrist at the end of the seven years preceding the Millennial Kingdom (**Revelation 19**). It is only by being *previously* resurrected and 'caught up' that the Bride can then be with him on his return.

If, on the other hand, the 'day' is *after* the Tribulation, but there is no Millennial Kingdom, then we are unable to explain why this future period of Christ's reign on earth has been such a feature of Revelation. Why was it alluded to many times in the Old Testament? These allusions provide the only glimpse of how God will deal with Satan.

In addition, the post-Tribulation need for sorting 'the sheep and the goats' (**Matthew 25:31-46**) would be redundant, as a post-Tribulation Rapture will have already accomplished the same job on the same day.

But Christ has indeed been raised from the dead, the firstfruits of those who have fallen asleep. For since death came through a man, the resurrection of the dead comes also through a man. For as in Adam all die, so in Christ all will be made alive. But each in his own turn: Christ, the firstfruits; then, when he comes, those who belong to him. Then the end will come, when he hands over the kingdom to God the Father after he has destroyed all dominion, authority and power. **For he must reign until** *he has put all his enemies under his feet. The last enemy to be destroyed is death.*

1 Corinthians 15:20-26

Within this highly relevant passage we recognise a clear chronological sequence of events. Christ will come, then he will take and resurrect those who belong to him, and then the end will come, during which '*he must reign until ...*'. In other words the resurrection of believers will **not** be on the *very* last day or 24 hours, it must occur some time before, and in between times Christ will reign until the last enemy is destroyed.

This passage helps verify the Millennial Kingdom of **Revelation 20:1-7** as well as provide evidence that the resurrection of believers occurs well *before* the very last day. All of this suggests that the resurrection '*at the last day*' refers either to the Rapture, to the Glorious Appearing, or is a time frame which is longer than a literal day and includes both of these.

To state that Christ's words '*at the last day*' literally meant the very last 24 hours, creates many problems across a whole variety of interpretations. As the details become examined such a belief becomes untenable.

Therefore we need to return to considering what '*the last day*' was actually referring to. So far we could argue that it may refer to the Glorious Appearing, or to the Rapture. It cannot be referring to the final 24-hours on earth prior to the creation of the new earth and new Heaven if a futurist interpretation of Revelation is to be maintained.

The natural alternative argument would be to consider again whether it refers to a period of time at which God's story will be brought to a close. Our study of the word '*hour*' in **Matthew 24:44** shows that in this context it does not refer to a period of 60 minutes, but to a season of time In the same way '*the last day*' may be referring to an era within the end-times. There is much to support this view, but it is perhaps most appropriate to argue from the premise of one of these same verses from John's Gospel in which '*the last day*' is mentioned.

There is a judge for the one who rejects me and does not accept my words; that very word which I spoke will condemn him at the last day.

John 12:48

We can see that '*the last day*' is not merely used to describe a day of resurrection for believers, but here it is used to describe the day of judgment for non-believers too.

While non-believers who are alive at the Glorious Appearing will be judged prior to the Millennial Kingdom, those who have died already will not be resurrected until the Great White Throne judgment which occurs right at the end of time (**Revelation 20:11-15**), after the Millennial Kingdom. This is the last thing to happen before the new heaven is introduced. This verse, then, refers to the day of judgment more than 1,000 years after Christ's Glorious Appearing, and further still after the Rapture. Yet we have seen how '*the last day*' can refer to each of these three events.

For all of the above reasons, then, I believe that Jesus' use of the term '*at the last day*' refers to that final period of time in which all matters regarding the resurrection and judgment shall be concluded.

3 What comes first, antichrist or Rapture?

Concerning the coming of our Lord Jesus Christ and our being gathered to him, we ask you, brothers, not to become easily unsettled or alarmed by some prophecy, report or letter supposed to have come from us, saying that the day of the Lord has already come. Don't let anyone deceive you in any way, for that day will not come until the rebellion occurs and the man of lawlessness is revealed, the man doomed to destruction. He will oppose and will exalt himself over everything that is called God or is worshipped, so that he sets himself up in God's temple, proclaiming himself to be God.

2 Thessalonians 2:1-4

In this short response we return to a key letter from Paul to the Thessalonians. Opposition to the pre-Tribulation theory has included use of the above text by claiming that if *'our being gathered to him'* is referring to the Rapture (verse 1), then it evidently will not occur until after *'the man of lawlessness is revealed'* (verse 3). This can be answered by drawing attention to the fact that Paul is not referring to *'that day'* (verse 3) as being the same as when we are *'gathered to him'*, but instead it refers to *'the day of the Lord'* (verse 2). It is the *'day of the Lord'* which will not occur until the *'man of lawlessness is revealed'*. If we concentrate on the subjects within the passage and extract them this matter is clarified for us: *'the day of the Lord ... will not come until ... the man of lawlessness is revealed'*.

We also note within this same passage that the readers had started to believe that *'the day of the Lord'* had already come. Evidently, then, they believed that *'the day of the Lord'* would last for longer than a literal 24 hours, but referred instead to a period of time which they thought had already arrived. This merely adds further support to the notion that *'the last day'* may similarly have a broader meaning than a single period of 24 hours, and lends weight to our previous response.

Finally, the fact that they thought *'the day of the Lord'* had already come would imply that they thought the Rapture had already occurred and they were worried that they might have missed it. The alternative is that they thought Christ had Gloriously Appeared already, which is highly unlikely as everyone will see him. Therefore, this argument provides further evidence for pre-Tribulation Rapture.

4 Should we be preparing Christians for the Tribulation?

If a pre-Tribulation Rapture is not imminent, and indeed is not biblical, then it could be argued that books such as this one ought to be preparing Christians for the trials that will be faced through the future time of Tribulation.

This book is focused on the Rapture precisely because it is endeavouring to find out whether such an event is biblical, and whether it can indeed occur at any moment.

So preparation for the Tribulation will only be necessary if we conclude that the pre-Tribulation Rapture idea is *not* scripturally valid.

On the other hand, we might draw conclusions from the same argument in reverse. Because the Bible does *not* appear to prepare Christians for the wrath of God as it unfolds in the Tribulation period, we can assume that this is because Christians will not be here to endure it.

Further biblical considerations

The following are some further references and arguments from Scripture which may be interpreted in the light of Rapture thinking, and are therefore worth consideration.

1 What are we waiting for?

We know that the whole creation has been groaning as in the pains of childbirth right up to the present time. Not only so, but we ourselves, who have the firstfruits of the Spirit, groan inwardly as we wait eagerly for our adoption as sons, the redemption of our

bodies. For in this hope we were saved. But hope that is seen is no
hope at all. Who hopes for what he already has? But if we hope for
what we do not yet have, we wait for it patiently.

Romans 8:22-25

Rather than be waiting *'eagerly'* for death, it is possible that this
passage has overtones of a belief in an imminent Rapture
behind it, and may also hint that Paul thought it could be in his
lifetime.

2 Who are we watching for?

*Be patient, then, brothers, until the Lord's coming. See how the
farmer waits for the land to yield its valuable crop and how patient
he is for the autumn and spring rains. You too, be patient and
stand firm, because the Lord's coming is near. Don't grumble
against each other, brothers, or you will be judged. The Judge is
standing at the door!*

James 5:7-9

Only the pre-Tribulation Rapture concept concurs with the belief
that we are watching patiently for *'the Lord's coming'*. All other
Rapture theories would have us wait for the antichrist, the
confirmation of the seven-year covenant and the subsequent
wrath in the Tribulation.

3 Heaven is our home

*But our citizenship is in Heaven. And we eagerly await a Saviour
from there, the Lord Jesus Christ, who, by the power that enables
him to bring everything under his control, will transform our lowly
bodies so that they will be like his glorious body.*

Philippians 3:20, 21

140

Heaven is our home, and Christ will come and transform our lowly bodies into heavenly ones. Again, though not substantial in itself, this passage is an interesting addition to our key texts, and if read in expectancy of an imminent Rapture it becomes all the more meaningful.

It is worth remembering that during the Millennial Kingdom, after Christ's Glorious Appearing, the inhabitants will have bodies which are subject to decay and death, though this may be over longer periods of time.

Never again will there be in it an infant who lives but a few days, or an old man who does not live out his years; he who dies at a hundred will be thought a mere youth; he who fails to reach a hundred will be considered accursed.

Isaiah 65:20

In comparing these two passages, then, we have further evidence for a pre-Tribulation Rapture, as for Christ to give believers glorious heavenly bodies at his Glorious Appearing would conflict with the bodies which inhabit the subsequent thousand-year Kingdom.

Instead, we may conclude that these words in Paul's letter to the Philippians indicate that the next event which we are eagerly anticipating is the Saviour's act of transforming his people's bodies into heavenly ones and taking us home!

4 Did Isaiah foresee the pre-Tribulation Rapture?

But your dead will live; their bodies will rise.
You who dwell in the dust, wake up and shout for joy.
Your dew is like the dew of the morning; the earth will give birth to her dead.

141

Go, my people, enter your rooms and shut the doors behind you;
hide yourselves for a little while until his wrath has passed by.
See, the LORD is coming out of his dwelling to punish the people of
the earth for their sins. The earth will disclose the blood shed upon
her; she will conceal her slain no longer.

Isaiah 26:19-21

If this passage is read within its context there is a good likelihood
that these words prophesied a future Rapture. Note that *'your*
dead' refers to those who belong to God, and that they *'will rise'*.
Therefore this is clearly not referring to the resurrection of
unbelievers at the end of time.

Note also that verse 20 fits in with the pre-Tribulation ideas of
being taken to heaven to enter heavenly *'rooms'*, and that this
move takes place before God's wrath comes (see *John 14:2-3* and
1 Thessalonians 1:10, Romans 5:9. We notice that after this
resurrection, and after entering the rooms, the Lord comes to
punish the sinful.

This passage certainly seems to reflect the pre-Tribulation Rapture
idea of resurrection and Rapture, followed by wrath, and then the
Glorious Appearing of Christ.

5 Another Rapture-type event?

I know a man in Christ who fourteen years ago was caught up to
the third heaven. Whether it was in the body or out of the body I
do not know – God knows. And I know that this man – whether in
the body or apart from the body I do not know, but God knows –
was caught up to paradise. He heard inexpressible things, things
that man is not permitted to tell.

2 Corinthians 12:2-4

In all probability Paul was talking about himself in this passage. It does not matter whether he was actually *'caught up'* in his body or whether it was in his spirit. One way or the other, Paul was in *'paradise'*.

But what really *does* matter, and what makes this passage so potentially substantial, is that Paul **believed** that his body and/or his spirit *could* be caught up to Heaven in such a way. This passage leaves no doubt that in the understanding of Paul – one of the greatest Old Testament scholars, New Testament authors, Christian missionaries, and early Church Messianic Jews – the Rapture was a possibility.

He firmly believed that he *may* have been caught up bodily. Even if that was not the case, if it was *'apart from the body'*, he nonetheless affirmed that he had experienced a Rapture-type event.

The fact that Paul believed that such a Rapture was possible, and openly shared this belief, adds yet further weight to teaching the validity of the future Rapture.

6 The obvious must not be forgotten

The angel said to me, 'These words are trustworthy and true. The Lord, the God of the spirits of the prophets, sent his angel to show his servants the things that must soon take place.'
'Behold, I am coming soon! Blessed is he who keeps the words of the prophecy in this book.'

Revelation 22:6, 7

Throughout this book the pre-Tribulation Rapture concept has been examined according to its scriptural validity, and while some arguments have been very plain and straightforward, others have been rather detailed. In all this, it is vital that the obvious truths are not forgotten. One of these is that the world will not continue as it is forever.

We are a part of God's story for humankind and at a time of his choosing he *will* bring it all to a close, and begin a new story, that of Heaven.

It sounds obvious, but it is on this clear teaching from the Bible that we legitimise our study, which is not 'whether' God will bring all things to a conclusion, nor is it a study of 'when', but it is a sincere and valid study of 'how'.

Surely the Sovereign LORD does nothing without revealing his plan to his servants the prophets.

Amos 3:7

7 It makes sense

While this section has attempted to examine the biblical rationale and considerations regarding the pre-Tribulation Rapture concept, it is worth contemplating the problems which might exist if such a theory were to be discarded.

First and foremost, we would have immense difficulty in making sense of our key texts.

Brothers, we do not want you to be ignorant about those who fall asleep, or to grieve like the rest of men, who have no hope. We believe that Jesus died and rose again and so we believe that God will bring with Jesus those who have fallen asleep in him. According to the Lord's own word, we tell you that we who are still alive, who are left till the coming of the Lord, will certainly not precede those who have fallen asleep. For the Lord himself will come down from Heaven, with a loud command, with the voice of the archangel and with the trumpet call of God, and the dead in Christ will rise first. After that, we who are still alive and are left will be caught up together with them in the clouds to meet the Lord in the air. And so we will be with the Lord forever. Therefore encourage each other with these words.

1 Thessalonians 4:13-18

Listen, I tell you a mystery: We will not all sleep, but we will all be changed – in a flash, in the twinkling of an eye, at the last trumpet. For the trumpet will sound, the dead will be raised imperishable, and we will be changed.

1 Corinthians 15:51-52

Do not let your hearts be troubled. Trust in God; trust also in me. In my Father's house are many rooms; if it were not so, I would have told you. I am going there to prepare a place for you. And if I go and prepare a place for you, I will come back and take you to be with me that you also may be where I am.

John 14:1-3

Unless there is going to be a Rapture as previously described then these passages, and the dozens which we have used to support them, become a cause for confusion, and lack meaning.

We would have to conclude that the next event within God's story is not the pre-Tribulation Rapture, but is the rise of the man of lawlessness, followed by the confirmation of a covenant with Israel, and seven years of extreme hardship and persecution. The best hope for the future of the Church would be to wait for these things, endure God's wrath, and then, if still alive, be thankful for his Glorious Appearing. The future without a pre-Tribulation Rapture would have us waiting eagerly for the antichrist, rather than watching for Christ.

We would be utterly confused about the meaning of passages which tell us that we do not know when Christ will come. Without a pre-Tribulation Rapture the opposite would be true, and at the very least we would know the vague season of his coming because it must follow those things listed above.

We would know that from the time the antichrist breaks his future covenant there will be just three and a half years until the Glorious Appearing (***Daniel 9:24-27; Revelation 13:5***). The idea of being *'caught up'* while working our normal everyday lives would be highly unlikely, for if we knew for certain that Christ would return within the next days, weeks, months, or even years, it is far more likely that the daily routines would cease.

Two men will be in the field; one will be taken and the other left. Two women will be grinding with a hand mill; one will be taken and the other left. Therefore keep watch, because you do not know on what day your Lord will come.

Matthew 24:40-42

It is unthinkable that the antichrist would be able to rule, blaspheme God, slander those in Heaven, and deceive the nations to fight against Jesus himself, if the Church were still around and therefore able to reveal his identity, affect his popularity, and even anticipate his actions through prophecy. A pre-Tribulation, pre-antichrist Rapture would surely be necessary for him to hold such authority. In addition to which, if there is no pre-Tribulation Rapture then it makes one wonder why the Bible does not offer any guidance for getting through those years of wrath, and even makes promises of deliverance not only meaningless but rather cruel in themselves.

So we argue that the pre-Tribulation Rapture concept not only has plentiful and substantial biblical support, but that disregarding it would be to create a confusing tangle of Scriptural prophecies and teachings and leave the believer without sufficient answers, and without future hope.

Conclusion

This section has attempted to provide a variety of arguments which are based on Scripture and which support the theory of a pre-Tribulation Rapture of the Church. In so doing it has presented a New Testament rationale, an Old Testament rationale, as well as various other additional considerations, including responses to counter-arguments.

In concluding this section, then, we have seen how these arguments have been varied in strength and weight, with some being more persuasive than others. The Old Testament rationale while confirming a futurist interpretation of Revelation, has a significant amount of speculation attached to it. Whether the Feast Day of Trumpets does indeed foreshadow a pre-Tribulation Rapture may not be evident until it happens.

Certainly the former feasts have evident prophetic meaning and fulfilment in events that have already passed. It would, therefore, be reasonable to assume that the 'next prophetic feast' within *Leviticus 23* also corresponds to the 'next event' within God's story.

We have seen the way in which Paul displays a knowledge of the prophetic nature of Leviticus 23, identifies the relationship between Adam and Christ, the importance of resurrection theology, and goes on to write a key Rapture text all within one chapter of a letter (*1 Corinthians 15*). This all adds up to a probability that Paul also saw the Day of Trumpets as being the foreshadow of the Rapture. However, a 'probability' is the only way to define this rationale.

In contrast, the New Testament rationale is very strong and persuasive. It is clear that the letters of the Bible must be given extra care as they are often written in response to something or someone. They are usually part of a conversation that has been taking place. Therefore we have tried to discover the theology which lies behind them, and we are grateful for the clues provided within Scripture which enable us to do this.

The line of reasoning beginning from the key texts is enough to affirm that the pre-Tribulation Rapture concept is scripturally valid, and that the Apostle Paul certainly seems to have both believed and taught this doctrine.

We can add to this persuasive New Testament rationale the other elements we have mentioned. These are:

- the further biblical considerations,
- the Old Testament rationale,
- our preliminary work on establishing the plausibility of a future transformation and expectation of God's next event on his prophetic calendar within his story.

Put together, these mean that the idea of pre-Tribulation Rapture of the Church becomes a truly formidable article of faith.

The doctrine of the pre-Tribulation Rapture of the Church is not an 'essential' doctrine. It is negotiable in that if Bible-students disagree on the matter then it makes no difference to our salvation or recognition of Jesus Christ. We may simply and gracefully disagree on this subject, agree on others, but ultimately look forward to greeting each other one day in Heaven. In the meantime, Bible-based and Spirit-led discussion and interpretation has to be a healthy thing.

The doctrine of a pre-Tribulation Rapture of the Church is biblically sound, It is stronger than its opposition, and Christians throughout the Church age can look forward in hope to being 'caught up' by their Lord to Heaven, where they will be united with those who have died in Christ. This truly is the 'next event'.

Whether this occurs sooner or later, while we are living or have long since died, we do not know. What we *do* know is that according to this concept the Rapture can happen at any moment.

The Rapture relevance

It is possible that readers of this book may question the relevance of studying such eschatological themes as the Rapture. It is equally possible that this book will challenge its readers to articulate its relevance to others.

It may be argued that to consider a future event which may or may not happen within our lifetime (or indeed for another 2,000 years) may appear to lack relevance to the here and now. This is so because the ideas have created differences of opinion, none of which can be proved to be without flaw, and all of which require a deliberate study of interrelated biblical texts.

It is my hope that, despite the differences of opinion, this book has enabled the reader to get to the heart of the debate. I hope readers will understand the most solid arguments for the Rapture, will study the necessary texts and at the very least will appreciate that such an event is biblically prophesied and doctrinally sound.

With regard to the *relevance* of the Rapture, this comes precisely from the recognition that we can never set dates or even predict in which generation this event will transpire. The evidence that leads us to adhere to the pre-Tribulation Rapture concept is the same evidence which is highlighting the fact that this event will be **continually** relevant until the day it occurs.

With both the mid-Tribulation and post-Tribulation Rapture concepts we can acknowledge that such study may not be relevant until 'nearer the time'. But with the pre-Tribulation Rapture theory, we know 'the time' is imminent, and there is nothing to stop the Rapture from occurring before the reader finishes this sentence. This makes the study of the Rapture more relevant than our next meal. Our study has led us to this point very carefully, providing evidence based on Scripture alone all the way.

Further to this unique, yet *general* relevance which is found within the pre-Tribulation Rapture concept, there is also the intensely *personal* relevance to consider. The implications relate to every individual.

They can be divided into three parts. First there is the necessity of faith in Jesus Christ, second there is the urgency of salvation, and third there is the obligation of holiness.

The necessity of faith in Jesus Christ

In my Father's house are many rooms; if it were not so, I would have told you. I am going there to prepare a place for you. And if I go and prepare a place for you, I will come back and take you to be with me that you also may be where I am.

John 14:2, 3

The above text is part of a passage which Jesus spoke regarding something that he will personally do. We might legitimately interpret the above for present-day Christians as: *In Jesus' Father's house are many rooms; if it were not so, Jesus would have told us. Jesus went there to prepare a place for us. And if Jesus has gone and prepared a place for us, Jesus will come back and take us to be with him that we also may be where Jesus is.*

Jesus spoke these words to his followers, and when they questioned how they can be sure to be counted among those who will go to be with Jesus, he replies, just a couple of verses on:

152

*I am the way and the truth and the life. No one comes to the Father
except through me.*

John 14:6

From these closely related texts we can see that faith in Jesus
Christ is not an option for inclusion in the Rapture. Neither is
faith in Jesus Christ an option for being reconciled to God the
Father. Faith in Jesus Christ is a requirement. It is a necessity. This
absolute truth may be observed in the other key Rapture texts too.

*Listen, I tell you a mystery: We will not all sleep, but we will all be
changed – in a flash, in the twinkling of an eye, at the last
trumpet. For the trumpet will sound, the dead will be raised
imperishable, and we will be changed. For the perishable must
clothe itself with the imperishable, and the mortal with
immortality.*

1 Corinthians 15:51-53

Although this was written to Christians, and the preceding
passage within the chapter has its focus on Jesus Christ, the best
demonstration of the Christ-centred nature of the Rapture from
this text would be to continue reading the following verses.

*When the perishable has been clothed with the imperishable, and
the mortal with immortality, then the saying that is written will
come true: 'Death has been swallowed up in victory.'*
'Where, O death, is your victory?
Where, O death, is your sting?'
*The sting of death is sin, and the power of sin is the law. But
thanks be to God! He gives us the victory through our Lord Jesus
Christ.*

1 Corinthians 15:54-57

The *'victory'* is for *'us'*, as opposed to belonging to death,
because of the resurrection and Rapture. Paul thanks God for it,

but specifically makes it clear that this victory can only be ours *'through our Lord Jesus Christ'*. Again, then, we see that inclusion in the future Rapture necessitates faith in Jesus Christ. Without such faith, we do not have the victory that the Bible speaks of.

For the Lord himself will come down from Heaven, with a loud command, with the voice of the archangel and with the trumpet call of God, and the dead in Christ will rise first. After that, we who are still alive and are left will be caught up together with them in the clouds to meet the Lord in the air. And so we will be with the Lord forever. Therefore encourage each other with these words.

1 Thessalonians 4:16-18

In the third of these key texts upon which the Rapture concept is built we have no need to look beyond the immediate passage. In this letter we have the matter sealed conclusively with the evidence that it is the *'dead in Christ'* who will be resurrected. In other words, Paul is referring to those who have placed their faith in Christ, but have died before the Rapture takes place. We also notice that within these three verses alone, the Lord Jesus Christ is referred to four times, as he is so intrinsic to the event. Once again, it is evident that faith in the Lord Jesus Christ is a requirement for inclusion in the Rapture.

Through a simple glimpse at these three texts we can confirm the necessity of faith in Jesus in order to be included among those who are 'caught up' at the Rapture.

When these three passages are combined the argument strengthens. The more Rapture-relevant Scripture texts we consider, the more obvious this statement becomes. We can declare from our key texts alone that the Rapture only includes those who have placed their faith in Jesus Christ.

What does this mean?

Placing our faith in Jesus Christ means we have acknowledged that God is pure and holy (for example **Leviticus 19:2**) and humankind is not. It is because each of us has sinned (for example **Romans 3:23**) – we have acted, spoken or thought in ways inconsistent with God's holiness – that we know we have fallen short of his standard. For us to live with the one Holy God would be impossible (for example **Hebrews 12:14**). Holiness no longer remains holy if it is infiltrated or tainted by sinfulness.

Therefore God, in an act of eternal love, came and died for us. He allowed his holy nature to be sacrificed in place of our sinfulness, so that everyone who places their trust in Jesus Christ's death for the forgiveness of sin can be assured that, in God's eyes, they are considered holy.

For God so loved the world that he gave his one and only Son, that whoever believes in him shall not perish but have eternal life.
John 3:16

This gift of salvation is available to everyone, and so is universally inclusive, but it is available only through trusting purely in the loving self-sacrifice made by Jesus Christ.

Salvation is found in no one else, for there is no other name under Heaven given to men by which we must be saved.
Acts 4:12

Just as salvation is available only through faith in Jesus Christ, because of the loving grace of God, so the resurrection and Rapture of believers is assured by the example of Christ's own resurrection. Jesus Christ alone has the authority to say *'I am the resurrection and the life'* (**John 11:25**), which he then proved, and so when he promises to come back for those who belong to

155

him we have no reason to doubt him, and every reason to believe him.

This means Christians should have absolutely no fear about the Rapture. It is the fulfilment of a promise of Jesus Christ, and something which we are to anticipate eagerly. The pre-Tribulation Rapture concept is the only one which teaches such a joyful future hope.

The personal relevance of the pre-Tribulation Rapture, then, includes the realisation that it is necessary to place our trust in Jesus Christ alone for our salvation, in order to be included among those who are 'caught up' to him. By implication, trust in anything or anyone else will lead to disappointment. Meanwhile, Christians can look forward to the return of their Lord and Saviour, in the hope and knowledge that he could return at any moment.

The urgency of salvation

We have emphasised the necessity of salvation in order to be
included in the Rapture. We have also emphasised the need for
that salvation to be based on faith in Jesus Christ alone, as only
he can reconcile us to God. It is for this reason that 'the next
event' is often specifically called the Rapture *of the Church*.
However, the pre-Tribulation Rapture concept teaches that there
are no further events, prophecies, or conditions which need to be
fulfilled before the Rapture takes place. This teaching makes it
unique among Rapture theories in that it is the only one which
places a pure focus on the Messiah Jesus.

It makes complete sense for the Christian to conclude that if the
Rapture is only for Christians, *and* it is imminent, then there
should be an added urgency within the Church to see the gospel
message of salvation shared appropriately at every opportunity.
Furthermore, it makes sense for the Church to be unafraid of
sending out a clear undiluted gospel invitation, and likewise for
individuals to take every appropriate opportunity to introduce
people to Jesus.

After 2,000 it is easy to understand how the Church may feel such
urgency may be exaggerated, but when we think that today may
be the last day available for friends, family members and loved
ones to be included in the Rapture of the Church, then the
urgency returns. The Rapture, imminent as it is, may be hundreds
of years away, but I have yet to meet a Christian who has
regretted their decision to place their trust in Christ. Surely there
is no such thing as a 'premature Christian', and the sooner we are
'born again' (*John 3:3*) through faith in Jesus Christ, the better,
even if the Rapture is centuries away.

If we adopt this state of considered urgency in our personal and
corporate proclamation of salvation, in the light of his imminent

return, then there are many eternal benefits. But if we are apathetic toward such an urgency then the consequences may well be disastrous not only for those who have yet to encounter Christ, who will miss the Rapture or, worse still, die without knowing him, but also for ourselves if we fail to recognise our responsibility.

Everyone who calls on the name of the Lord will be saved. How, then, can they call on the one they have not believed in? And how can they believe in the one of whom they have not heard? And how can they hear without someone preaching to them? And how can they preach unless they are sent? As it is written, 'How beautiful are the feet of those who bring good news!'

Romans 10:13-15

We need to ask the Holy Spirit to increase our zeal and desire to bring this good news to those around us; friends, colleagues, our community, and those closest to us. How terrible it would be for our loved ones not to take seriously God's gift of salvation, simply because we were never serious about sharing the good news. On the other hand, how fulfilling it would be to know that we are doing what we can to spread the gospel. How wonderful it would be for those around us to consider seriously God's free gift. How joyful it will be when we are reunited with loved ones who have accepted Jesus Christ as their Saviour, and we are gathered together with them at his coming.

God loves us so much that he gave us freewill to choose whether to accept or reject his Son, Jesus Christ. We would not ever try to coerce someone into accepting salvation, even if the intention was for their eternal benefit. However, we can influence the degree of seriousness with which those around us consider him, by sharing the gospel in appropriate and sensitive ways that will express our loving concern. Ultimately it is the individual's choice, but the imminence of a pre-Tribulation Rapture reminds us that there ought to always be an element of urgency in getting the message of salvation heard.

If you confess with your mouth, 'Jesus is Lord' and believe in your heart that God raised him from the dead, you will be saved. For it is with your heart that you believe and are justified, and it is with your mouth that you confess and are saved.

Romans 10:9,10

Seek the LORD while he may be found; call on him while he is near.

Isaiah 55:6

The obligation of holiness

For it is by grace you have been saved, through faith – and this not from yourselves, it is the gift of God – not by works, so that no one can boast. For we are God's workmanship, created in Christ Jesus to do good works, which God prepared in advance for us to do.

Ephesians 2:8-10

The pre-Tribulation Rapture concept includes an intrinsic truth regarding its relevance in that it brushes aside any claim to salvation which is not based on faith alone in Jesus Christ. It also adds urgency to the proclamation of such salvation as described in the previous chapter. The third major relevance pertaining to this theory is the need, or obligation of holiness.

Quite simply, holiness – striving to be the people God wants us to be – goes hand in hand with salvation. It is not salvation itself, but it should be a direct and immediate result of being saved.

Since we have these promises, dear friends, let us purify ourselves from everything that contaminates body and spirit, perfecting holiness out of reverence for God.

2 Corinthians 7:1

There are many references within the Bible to the manner in which we are saved. The whole theme running throughout the New Testament is how Jesus Christ has paid the price of salvation for us, and that through him we are reconciled with God. It is because of Christ's atoning work on the cross, his perfect sacrifice, that we have no need whatsoever to try and earn our salvation. In fact, if we try and perform any rituals, deeds, or works with the aim of gaining salvation then we evidently are not putting our faith solely in Christ at all, and have missed the point of what he has already accomplished for us.

160

One such Bible reference is found in Paul's letter to the Ephesians which combines all three facets to salvation within these three verses. We are not saved by works, we are saved by God's grace through faith, but then Paul adds: *'For we are God's workmanship, created in Christ Jesus to do good works, which God prepared in advance for us to do'* (**Ephesians 2:10**).

While salvation can in no way be earned, but relies solely on our trust in what Christ has already done, there should nevertheless be a natural by-product whereby Christians will be eager to do what God wants us to do, and to be who he wants us to be.

But now that you have been set free from sin and have become slaves to God, the benefit you reap leads to holiness, and the result is eternal life.

Romans 6:22

A simple illustration would be to consider a footballer who used to play for Sinful City, but has transferred his allegiance to a new team, Holiness United. The signing of a new contract immediately brings that player into a new team, with new tactics and a new manager. Similarly, at the point of salvation Christ's death makes us holy in God's sight as we place ourselves under his blood through faith, but the automatic response should be to strive to live a holy life too. For this we have been given the gift of the Holy Spirit to guide our thoughts and instincts.

The call to holiness, then, is not an option. It is an automatic by-product of salvation, instigated by our response to Christ and aided by the indwelling of the Holy Spirit. However, the degree to which we are willing to submit to the Holy Spirit's guidance certainly *is* optional, as he will not coerce anyone or force us to live as God desires. Once again, God's love is supreme. The decision exists, then, as to whether Christians are to consider

161

Jesus Christ merely as their Saviour, or whether he is our Lord as well, to whom we submit.

The pre-Tribulation Rapture concept brings an emphasis upon this obligation of holiness. It asks the Church to consider how it has responded to the call to holiness which every Christian hears from the moment they accept Jesus Christ as Saviour. It highlights the fact that Christ could return literally at any moment, and, though saved, all Christians will be rewarded according to the degree to which they have responded to the Holy Spirit's guidance (*1 Corinthians 3:10-16*).

If we expect Christ to be pleased with our lives, then we need to strive toward lives of holiness. If we believe that Christ could return at any moment, we need to start such striving for holiness immediately.

It is for exactly this reason, and the inseparable link between salvation and the subsequent call to holiness, that we would expect to find evidence of the obligation of holiness in relation to our Rapture texts. Such evidence is plentiful, and a considerable example is now provided.

The key texts

The key texts for the Rapture concept are fully consistent with our assertion that, having accepted God's gift of salvation, we should now be striving for holiness in anticipation of Christ's imminent return.

To start with, our key text from *1 Thessalonians 4:13-18* is preceded by these words:

Finally, brothers, we instructed you how to live in order to please God, as in fact you are living. Now we ask you and urge you in the

Lord Jesus to do this more and more. For you know what
instructions we gave you by the authority of the Lord Jesus.
It is God's will that you should be sanctified: that you should avoid
sexual immorality; that each of you should learn to control his own
body in a way that is holy and honorable, not in passionate lust
like the heathen, who do not know God; and that in this matter no
one should wrong his brother or take advantage of him. The Lord
will punish men for all such sins, as we have already told you and
warned you.
For God did not call us to be impure, but to live a holy life.
Therefore, he who rejects this instruction does not reject man but
God, who gives you his Holy Spirit.

1 Thessalonians 4:1-8

These verses clearly substantiate this chapter's claim that
Christians have an obligation of holiness: *'It is God's will that you
should be sanctified.'* The last two sentences in particular
emphasise this same message, and yet this whole passage comes
almost immediately before the first of our key Rapture texts. This
is because the one goes hand in hand with the other. They are
inseparable. We are to be sanctified, set apart and living holy
lives, out of loving reverence for God and in the knowledge that
Christ may return at any moment. It is because the Rapture is the
next event, with nothing requiring prophetic fulfilment
beforehand, that our lives should all the more eagerly
demonstrate our anticipation of, and readiness for, his coming, by
being pure and striving toward holiness.

The second key text of *1 Corinthians 15:50-54* is not as
wonderfully blatant about the need for holiness as the above
passage, but yet it too has a natural addition to the main teaching
of the chapter. After explaining the need for believing in the
resurrection, and highlighting the future Rapture in this context,
Paul then closes the passage by saying:

Therefore, my dear brothers, stand firm. Let nothing move you. Always give yourselves fully to the work of the Lord, because you know that your labour in the Lord is not in vain.

1 Corinthians 15:58

The very word '*therefore*' implies that Paul is using this as a conclusion. He has provided an argument for the truth of the resurrection. He has explained how our heavenly bodies will differ from our earthly ones. He has outlined the order of the Rapture, which will demonstrate how our faith in Christ overcomes death. Then he concludes with the above sentences, reminding his readers to '*always give yourselves fully to the work of the Lord*'. This must surely refer to God's call to holiness, doing and being what he desires.

The last of our three key texts comes from **John 14:1-3**, which apparently caused a little confusion among the disciples. In the following verses Jesus clarifies his relationship with God the Father, asserts that no one can come to the Father except through the Son, before he provides the link between the Rapture and the need for holiness.

If you love me, you will obey what I command. And I will ask the Father, and he will give you another Counsellor to be with you forever – the Spirit of truth.

John 14:15-17

These words occur within the same conversation as our key text, and are recorded as being said just a few sentences later. Christ has just told them that he would be going away, but will come back for those who believe in him. Then he gives the instruction that in the meantime they are to obey him, because they love him, and declares that the Holy Spirit will help them. Once again this is another way of saying that Christians have an obligation of holiness, that we have the Holy Spirit to help us in our response

164

to this call, and that it is all within the context of Jesus coming back for his Church.

Other helpful comparisons

It has already been mentioned how the Church is considered to be the Bride, with Christ the Bridegroom, who are betrothed through the new covenant of salvation. There are various biblical and prophetic reasons why this suggestion is often accepted, but certainly **Ephesians 5:22-33** is a key passage in this respect. It talks about the relationship between husbands and wives, frequently referring to similarities between Christ and the Church, and then in verses 31, 32 we read:

For this reason a man will leave his father and mother and be united to his wife, and the two will become one flesh. This is a profound mystery – but I am talking about Christ and the church.
Ephesians 5:31, 32

With regard to the anticipation of Christ's return and our obligation of holiness, this description of the Church being Christ's wife becomes particularly relevant when we consider a specific portion of this same passage.

Husbands, love your wives, just as Christ loved the church and gave himself up for her to make her holy, cleansing her by the washing with water through the word, and to present her to himself as a radiant church, without stain or wrinkle or any other blemish, but holy and blameless.
Ephesians 5:25-27

Christ intends to present Christians to himself as being holy and blameless. The Bride ought to be busy preparing for the time when the Groom comes to collect her. In preparing ourselves to meet him, then, the obligation is for us to respond to the call to holiness with immediate effect, as he could return for us at any moment.

But we know that when he appears, we shall be like him, for we shall see him as he is. Everyone who has this hope in him purifies himself, just as he is pure.
Everyone who sins breaks the law; in fact, sin is lawlessness. But you know that he appeared so that he might take away our sins. And in him is no sin. No one who lives in him keeps on sinning. No one who continues to sin has either seen him or known him.

1 John 3:2b-6

These verses from a letter of John once again clearly reveal the link between salvation, the need for holiness, and the return of Christ. Our future hope requires a present striving for holiness.

In addition to these specific references in relation to the Church or the Rapture, the Bible as a whole is full of calls to holiness, and examples of those who have previously strived for such holy lives.

I will sing of your love and justice; to you, O LORD, I will sing praise. I will be careful to lead a blameless life – when will you come to me? I will walk in my house with blameless heart.

Psalm 101:1, 2

Such references may remind us that even without our assurance of salvation, holiness should be a goal of life out of pure reverence for the holy God. It is simply the 'right' thing to do. Of course, the problem is our inherent inability to maintain such a focus without slipping, intentionally or otherwise, which is why Jesus needed to die for us, and why we still need the Holy Spirit's help today.
As a penultimate comment on the need to be striving for holiness in anticipation of Christ's imminent return for his Church, it is worth just briefly reminding ourselves of the stories of Noah and

166

Lot. These characters were referred to by Jesus in **Matthew 24** and **Luke 17** as he taught about the end-time conditions preceding his return. Both of them escaped the judgment which came upon those around them. Both of them are mentioned by Peter in his letter (**2 Peter 2:4-9**) as being examples of how God knows how to rescue us from judgment. Both of them are often considered to be examples of how God will rescue the Church from his coming wrath.

Clearly decisions needed to be made by these characters. Lot needed to warn those he loved of the impending destruction of Sodom, and then to lead them out of harm's way to safety. With the angels' help, Lot responded to the message with faithful obedience. Similarly, Noah was a man who revered God, and when warned of the judgment that was about to come upon the earth he responded by obeying what God told him to do. He had to make preparations, and was faithfully obedient. If the parallels are continued, then, we could argue that the obligation of holiness for the Church is similar to the faithful obedience of these characters, and it typically precedes God's judgment upon the unrighteous.

Noah was a righteous man, blameless among the people of his time, and he walked with God.

Genesis 6:9

We may remind ourselves of Noah's description as a blameless, righteous man, and of these similarities with his predecessor, Enoch. Like Noah, Enoch is described as having '*walked with God*', which must be a phrase which any Christian would dearly love for people to use in describing them.

Enoch walked with God; then he was no more, because God took him away.

Genesis 5:18

With Enoch, this 'walk with God' is the last description we have of him before he is taken away in a Rapture-like event. The similarities to the future Rapture of the Church may be coincidental, but we contend that Enoch's example is the perfect illustration of the Church's future obligation and hope. His life and departure foreshadows the necessity of faith, the imminence of being 'taken away', and the obligation of holiness in the meantime, as we strive, through the Holy Spirit's help, to live in a way that is pleasing to God.

By faith Enoch was taken from this life, so that he did not experience death; he could not be found, because God had taken him away. For before he was taken, he was commended as one who pleased God.

Hebrew 11:5

In the knowledge of the imminent Rapture, and out of loving reverence to God, may we be ready for him, preparing for him, striving toward holiness, heeding the call to sanctification and being people who may rightly be described as they who *'walk with God'.*

May God himself, the God of peace, sanctify you through and through. May your whole spirit, soul and body be kept blameless at the coming of our Lord Jesus Christ.
The one who calls you is faithful and he will do it.

1 Thessalonians 5:23, 24

Conclusion

In concluding this section on the Rapture's relevance we can understand how the next prophetic event to occur, brings into sharp focus the necessity of faith in Jesus Christ, the urgency of salvation, and the obligation of holiness.

The pre-Tribulation Rapture concept is the only futurist eschatology which argues for an imminent return of Christ to collect his Church. All the other variations require some other prophecy or requirement to be fulfilled beforehand. Therefore this Rapture theory alone has the Church eagerly anticipating and waiting for Jesus Christ to come. Other theories await the appearance of other characters, or the occurrence of preceding events or circumstances.

The Rapture, then, is something for the Church to look forward to. It is not something for Christians to fear or dread. It is a future hope for all who have placed their faith in Jesus Christ. This concept is ultimately relevant because it consumes any fear of the future with hope.

The assertion that Christ could return at any moment brings with it an urgency for salvation, not only for ourselves to become reconciled with God, but also for the gospel message to be proclaimed widely, clearly, sensitively and appropriately, so as many people can share this future hope as possible. It encourages the urgent salvation of our loved ones, friends, colleagues, and strangers in the light of his imminent return.

The teaching of the imminent return of Jesus Christ for his Church also urges us to strive toward holiness. Such a way of life ought to be sought out of reverence for God, as well as love for him. It is the means by which many might be attracted to Christ. The call to holiness is an obligation, a natural result of salvation, but it is not a call which we have to try and work at on our own. We have the Holy Spirit to help and guide us. The call to holiness is heard by every Christian. In the knowledge that Christ could come back at any moment, the wise hear and act upon it, and 'walk with God'.

In three important ways, then, the pre-Tribulation Rapture concept maintains its extreme relevance to everyone, both inside and outside the Church.

Finally, however, we might also argue that with or without these vital aspects of its relevance, the Rapture is worth examining, for the simple reason that it gives us a further insight into God's story. It encourages the study and application of the Bible, and it confirms once again that God is Sovereign. The pre-Tribulation Rapture concept, then, is highly relevant if we allow it to be, but, like all Scripture, we have the choice of whether or not to respond to the Holy Spirit's leading.

And the answer is ...

This book has been produced as an attempt to consider the scriptural validity of the Rapture. As a natural by-product, it has also been an introduction to biblical eschatology, based upon a futurist interpretation of the relevant prophetic passages.

It is necessary for this highly debated doctrine to receive a significant and defined response, as greater numbers of people, both within the Church and without, are becoming aware of it. The increasingly popular Rapture ideas therefore need to be tested according to scriptural authority, and to find out whether they are both biblically valid and relevant.

In this study we have approached this crucial question regarding the Rapture concept's scriptural validity and relevance by methodically leading the reader through the key themes, texts and concepts in the hope that the Bible may be allowed to speak for itself. As a result, not only are we able to assess the persuasiveness of biblical texts for ourselves with regard to this doctrine, but we may also enjoy the blessing and spiritual nourishment which such study of Scripture provides.

To begin with, we set the eschatological scene, aware that such concepts can be rather confusing, unfamiliar, and even intimidating due to their apocalyptic nature and necessary cross-referencing. We provided definitions of key events and characters as well as outlining the rationale behind our chosen mode of interpretation. We then asserted that it is both legitimate and, to an extent, natural to consider what the 'next event' may be within God's prophetic calendar. If God's story has a beginning and an end, which precedes our eternity in Heaven, then even the casually curious may pause to consider at what stage or era within that story we are currently living in.

This, in turn, led us to consider how God has often used many dramatic, miraculous, direct and indirect means to establish his will within that story, and that the Rapture concept, therefore, may not be discounted on the basis of its scientific improbability. As such, it may be brought into the discussion as a possible 'next event'.

The Rapture concept was then outlined in detail, introducing the key texts for this doctrine, how it is normally kept distinct from the Glorious Appearing of Christ which is usually identified as the second coming, as well as providing biblical precedents which added a great deal of plausibility.

This brought us to consider the proposed timing of the Rapture, which is the main cause of disagreement regarding this theory. While acknowledging the validity and sincerity of opposing arguments, it was asserted that the pre-Tribulation Rapture view appears to be the strongest and most reliable, as well as the only one that teaches imminence regarding Christ's coming. If Christ can come at any moment, then the pre-Tribulation Rapture view must be the most likely.

So we focused on the pre-Tribulation proposition. We considered a New Testament rationale, which was very persuasive, based on the things Jesus said and the things Paul wrote. We also examined a very interesting Old Testament rationale, based on Leviticus 23, which, though not as persuasive, was certainly collaborative, truly affirming God's sovereignty, omniscience and efficiency. Finally we brought to the debate a large and substantial range of other biblical considerations, including responses to opposing views, all of which provided a scripturally holistic analysis of the pre-Tribulation Rapture concept's validity.

The doctrine of the pre-Tribulation Rapture of the Church is not an 'essential' doctrine. It is negotiable in that if Bible-students disagree on the matter it makes no difference to one's salvation or recognition of Jesus Christ. We may simply and gracefully disagree on this subject, agree on others, but ultimately look forward to greeting each other one day in Heaven.

However, the view of this book is that this doctrine *is* biblically sound, that it is stronger than its opposition, that Christians throughout the Church age can look forward in hope for the Rapture which will take them to Heaven, where they will be united with those who have died in Christ, and that this truly is the 'next event'.

We considered the present-day relevance of this concept, discovering the Rapture's focus on the necessity of having faith in Jesus Christ, the urgency of salvation, and the obligation of holiness. These are given unparalleled relevance when one considers that the Rapture could happen at any moment.

Until the Rapture occurs, the Church needs to be preparing herself, striving for holiness, and proclaiming with urgency the gospel of salvation, which is freely ours through faith in Jesus Christ alone. This statement of belief is for Christians individually and corporately. It should be true in all generations, present and future. But the scripturally valid Rapture concept teaches us that our window of opportunity to practise such a belief is by no means guaranteed to remain open. Christ may come for his Church today!

Amen. Come, Lord Jesus.
The grace of the Lord Jesus be with God's people. Amen.

Revelation 22:20, 21

If you would like to place your trust in Jesus Christ you can do so simply by speaking to God right now, where you are … he's listening!

Alternatively, below is a simple prayer which may be useful to you. God knows the intention of your heart.

A prayer for salvation

Dear Heavenly Father,
I admit that I am a sinner and need your forgiveness.
I believe that Jesus Christ died in my place, shedding his blood to pay for my sins, and that he rose again from the dead to assure me of eternal life.
I am willing right now to turn from my sin and accept Jesus Christ as my personal Saviour and Lord.
I commit my life to you and ask you to send the Holy Spirit into my life, to guide and control my thoughts and actions so that I can be the person you want me to be.
Thank you, Father, for loving me.
In Jesus' name, Amen.

If this is the first time you have sincerely prayed such a prayer and placed your trust in Jesus - congratulations! Welcome to the spiritual family of God. You are now a member of the Church! If we never get to meet here on earth, I look forward to seeing you in Heaven. You may well feel the Holy Spirit's urge to tell someone about your new/renewed faith. Don't resist it! I sincerely recommend that you find a warm, welcoming, spiritually sensitive and Christ-centred church, and that along with prayers you begin to read the Bible as a means of developing your relationship with God. The Gospel of John is a good place to start.

May God bless you, protect you and give you peace!

Bibliographical resources

Buksbazen, Victor, *The Gospel in the Feasts of Israel,*
   The Friends of Israel, New Jersey, 1954

Bullinger, E.W., *The Lord's Day*
   The Open Bible Trust, Reading, 2008

Chatham, Doug, *The Rapture Book,*
   Whitaker House, Pennsylvania, 1974

Ice, Thomas, and Demy, Timothy, *The Tribulation,*
   Harvest House Publishers, Oregon, 1996

LaHaye, Tim, *No Fear of the Storm,*
   New Wine Ministries, Chichester, 1992

Liberman, Paul, *The Fig Tree Blossoms: Messianic Judaism Emerges,*
   Fountain Press, Iowa, 1976

Walvoord, John F., *The Rapture Question,*
   Zondervan, Michigan, 1979

http://www.askmoses.com

http://endtimepilgrim.org/70wks3.htm

http://www.hebcal.com

http://www.jewishencyclopedia.com

http://www.rapturesolution.com

http://www.scook.org

http://www.torah.org